American
Woven
Coverlets

I dedicate this book
to the memory of my mother, Esther Sayles, who enjoyed
    hand-crafts and took great delight in "making things
    out of nothing,"
to my husband, Stewart Strickler, who has spent the last
    twenty years graciously resisting his natural urge to
    step on the accelerator instead of the brake when we
    approach an antique shop, and
to Mustie-Because-of-Her-Mustache, my feline assistant,
    who had the good sense to help with this book by
    lying on the manuscript and *not* on the coverlets.

I acknowledge and thank Deborah Robson for cheer-
ing me on with contagious enthusiasm when writing
bogged and wool coverlets seemed incompatible with
record summer heat.

I also offer my sincere appreciation to each of the
many, many antiques dealers, museum curators, coverlet
collectors, weavers, coverlet owners, friends, acquaint-
ances, and complete strangers who've generously shared
coverlet information with me over the years—without
you, this book wouldn't have been written! I thank you
all.

American Woven Coverlets

Carol Strickler

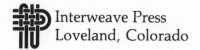
Interweave Press
Loveland, Colorado

Illustrations by Ann Sabin
Typesetting by Marc M. Owens
Cover by Signorella Graphic Arts

 Interweave Press
306 North Washington Avenue
Loveland, Colorado 80537

Library of Congress Catalog Number 87-80524
ISBN: 0-934026-30-0
First Printing: 5M:1187:ARC/CL

Library of Congress Cataloging-in-Publication Data
Strickler, Carol.
 American woven coverlets.

 Bibliography: p.
 Includes index.
 1. Hand weaving—United States. 2. Coverlets—United
States. I. Title.
TT848.S767 1987   746.9'0973   87-80524
ISBN 0-934026-30-0 (pbk.)

Introduction

In 1967 I learned to weave. A second-generation craft "dabbler," I soon found that textiles were the love I had been seeking all my life. Visits to family in Berea, Kentucky, strengthened my interest in traditional weaves and patterns. I learned to draw patterns on paper and "analyze" them to find out how they were woven. I learned that there were different weave structures with names like *overshot* and *summer & winter* and *double weave*. I learned that there were thousands of patterns that could be woven in these weaves, patterns determined by the way I threaded and treadled the loom.

And then, in 1971, an antique dealer friend put the spark to the tinder. She said, "I have this old cloth here that I thought you might find interesting. I think it's a piece of old bedspread or coverlet. It's in such bad shape that you may have it if you want—I'm just going to throw it out otherwise." Being frugal (and a magpie as well), I accepted the gift and began reading the few books available, to see what I could find out about it. Despite the fact that the cotton part was tattered practically out of existence, I was able to figure out that it was a fragment of a cotton-and-wool double weave coverlet or bedcover, probably woven by a professional weaver over 125 years before! When I returned to the dealer's shop to share what I'd learned, she gave me two additional, different, very tattered fragments that she had found in the meantime. (She sure knew how to keep a customer coming back!) Analysis told me these pieces were both overshot weave. Research told me their pattern names were "Catalpa Flower" and "Fox Trail." I learned that they were probably 150 years old and had been woven at home by women who had spun the wool and dyed it for pattern.

I was hooked! Here was a link with my cultural, domestic, and artistic past. I could hold in my hands a piece made by an unknown woman one-and-a-half centuries before, and by studying the piece itself I could find out everything I needed to know to make new fabric just like it. I would weave reproduction coverlets for a living!

Well, things didn't quite work out that way. It's been nearly twenty years, I'm still weaving, and I've made only one coverlet. But even though my weaving took other directions, my interest didn't. In those twenty years I've collected about a hundred coverlets and coverlet fragments, and have analyzed close to a thousand others. I've published, for weavers, five small loose-leaf volumes of coverlet analyses and information. I've spotted coverlets being used as car seat-covers and lampshades and curtains and stereo-speaker-cloth and couch-throws and backdrops for magazine articles on food. I've talked to weavers' guilds and antique-dealers' associations and DAR chapters and collectors' clubs and individual coverlet owners about the origins and care of coverlets. And when my own collection grew so large that speaking on care became a case of "do as I say, not as I do," I found a museum home for most of my best pieces.

The three questions I'm asked most frequently by coverlet owners are:
- "What do I have?"
- "How can I care for it?"
- "What is it worth?"

I can't answer that third question, because I am not an appraiser and because the value depends on widely variable factors, such as condition, weave structure, provenance, known history, and local market conditions. This book is a guide to the history and variety of coverlets made in the United States. (Canada's coverlet tradition, which in some respects closely parallels that of the U.S., has been comprehensively covered in Harold and Dorothy Burnham's 'Keep Me Warm One Night': Early Handweaving in Eastern Canada.) And there are ways an individual can handle a coverlet to preserve it. Consequently, I hope this book will help answer the first two questions.

I keep six honest serving-men
 (They taught me all I knew)
Their names are What and Why and When
And How and Where and Who.

R. Kipling: The Elephant's Child

JOE COCA

A coverlet is a handwoven cover for a bed. Its pattern is made as the cloth is woven. This red-and-white coverlet is in a weave structure called "summer & winter." It appears in color on pages 36 and 37, and a complete description can be found on pages 162–63.

What are coverlets?

With apologies to Kipling for rearrangement of his order, I'd like to put his serving-men to work on the subject of coverlets.

My dictionary defines coverlet as "an ornamental cloth covering for a bed." But I like to be a little narrower than that in my definition. As I use the word, a coverlet is "a hand-woven bedcover with loom-controlled pattern." This means that a coverlet was woven on a person-operated loom; it is one fabric (although it may be strips sewn together for greater width); and its pattern or decorative design was determined by the way the loom was threaded and treadled.

Some people call their coverlet a quilt, counterpane, bedspread, comforter, coverlid, or kivver. But a *quilt* is two or more separate fabrics put together as a sandwich (with or without filling) and stitched with lines of thread. A quilt's pattern may be formed by piecing of fabrics (patchwork or appliqué) or by embroidery or other surface embellishment. A *comforter* is, like a quilt, two or more separate fabrics sandwiched, but it is puffier and is only tied together at intervals instead of being closely stitched. *Counterpane* and *bedspread* are words that, to me, include other kinds of cloth bedcovers (such as chenille, tufted, and other weaver-controlled woven fabrics), covers

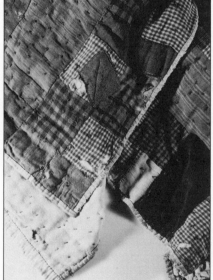

JOE COCA

embellished with embroidery (such as cross-stitch, crewel, trapunto, or candlewicking), and mill-woven spreads (such as the white marseille so popular in the late 19th century).

Of the above words only two mean what I mean when I say "coverlet"— *coverlid* is a variant of the word and *kivver* is Appalachian dialect. Originally all these terms probably derive from *couvre-lit*, French for "to cover the bed."

A comforter can serve some of the same functions as a coverlet, but is made by sewing together separate pieces of fabric. See far right of page 40 for a color view of this comforter.

Why were coverlets woven?

By definition, coverlets were woven to cover the beds. But the answer to this question has many aspects, some of which are surprising. Coverlets offered early American weavers an opportunity to make a fabric which was both practical (warm) and decorative.

Politics and economics influenced the textiles of early America, including coverlets. Before the Revolution, England had followed a policy of making her colonies dependent on her for manufactured goods, especially textiles. Colonial production was forbidden or severely restricted. In the decades before and after the Revolutionary War, England also controlled the export of textile mill equipment, jealously guarded knowledge of improvements, and forbade the emigration of anyone with the know-how to design, build, operate, or maintain such equipment. After the War she flooded the American former colonies with fabrics which were sold at prices lower than their European costs (prices substantially lower than cost of American manufacture), seriously undermining attempts to promote an American textile industry. Some of the aristocrats continued to wear and use the imported fabrics, which were finer and fancier. But even they soon realized that the new country was going to need *economic* as well as *political* independence. So in the early days of coverlet weaving all of these factors combined to make home production of household textiles a patriotic occupation.

In addition, fabrics were important possessions in those days among all classes of citizens. Textiles were listed in estate inventories and wills. They were a major factor in dowries. Creation of fabrics was a sign of a woman's domesticity and industry. Bedcoverings were a status symbol, and the more elaborate the better!

Above: *Laodicea ("Aunt Dicie") Fletcher, c. 1830-1913, winding handspun yarn from a high wheel onto a skeiner. The Fletcher family moved to Rugby, Tennessee, after the Civil War. They brought a loom with them, and Dicie Fletcher spent her life spinning, dyeing, and weaving. There's another picture of her on page 88.*
Below: *"Old time spinner living up in the mountains of Tennessee," a photograph by Lewis Hine.*

HISTORIC RUGBY ARCHIVES

GEORGE EASTMAN HOUSE

When were coverlets woven?

There are three key decades in the history of coverlets—the 1810s, the 1820s, and the 1860s.

Most of the old coverlets which still exist today were woven in the first half of the 19th century. Some coverlets were probably woven in the last quarter of the 18th century, but few of those have survived the ravages of wear, patching, re-use (as quilt filler or curtain liner or mattress pad) or recycling (into rags or paper). A coverlet woven before 1800 was probably made at home of handspun wool and linen. Flax cultivation, harvesting, preparation, and spinning are very time-intensive. The resulting linen was used primarily for other household fabrics, and relatively few linen-based coverlets were created—that, too, contributes to their present rarity. Published resources indicate that the earliest known dated coverlet is an overshot piece in the Winterthur Museum. It has a 1773 date and initials woven in.

In the early 19th century (especially in the economic aftermath of the War of 1812) textiles changed dramatically in the United States. Before that there had been ways of weaving faster (such as the fly-shuttle loom). There had been primitive ways of machine-spinning cotton yarn, but the yarn was too weak to use for warp and the preparation of cotton fibers had still been a very slow, hand-done, slave-labor job. In the 1790s the invention of an effective cotton gin (for removing the seeds from the cotton bolls by machine) broke the logjam of technology. Gins could prepare the fibers with sufficient speed and volume to supply the machines that carded, combed, and spun the cotton. Improvements in spinning equipment resulted in a yarn strong enough for warp, so that the new cotton could be woven into cloth. American factories soon produced household and clothing fabrics that quickly replaced homespun textiles. This freed the home loom for the

An early coverlet, of handspun wool (pattern), cotton (warp), and linen (weft). (Details on pages 124–25.)

12

COURTESY, THE HENRY FRANCIS DU PONT WINTERTHUR MUSEUM

This coverlet was found near Saugerties, New York, and is now located at The Henry Francis du Pont Winterthur Museum, in Winterthur, Delaware. A date in one corner indicates that it was made in 1773, which is unusually early for an American coverlet. The coverlet is made of a combination of handspun yarns — cotton, wool, and linen. A detail of the date-and-signature corner appears on page 90.

weaving of more decorative fabrics like coverlets. By 1810, American spinning mills were also producing the new cotton yarns for sale. Individual and professional weavers found the new yarns to be so inexpensive and readily available that they promptly quit using laboriously hand-spun linen and turned to mill-spun cotton for their coverlet weaving.

The hand-weaving of coverlets suddenly blossomed. Housewives traded (or jealously hoarded) their favorite patterns. Professional weavers built looms with more shafts and wove fancier patterns. The prime period of hand-woven coverlets extended from 1810 to the 1840s.

The next important happening in coverlet history was the importation of the first Jacquard loom mechanism from Europe in the mid-1820s. The Jacquard (named for its French inventor) is an apparatus that attaches to the upper part of a loom and replaces the shafts with individual heddles. It uses cords, rods, hooks, and punched cards to control the lifting of warp threads and formation of sheds for the wefts. Since each card has several hundred positions, a pattern can have several hundred warp threads operating independently. Very elaborate and pictorial patterns are possible with a Jacquard-equipped loom. Many professional weavers converted their looms with a Jacquard mechanism and suddenly the weaving of "fancy" coverlets replaced the home-weaving of simpler geometric patterns in some areas of the country. The 1830s, 1840s, and early 1850s were the heyday of Jacquard coverlet weaving.

The late 1850s and the decade around the Civil War saw the end of the era of coverlet weaving in the U.S. The Industrial Revolution had brought many improvements to the textile industry. The mills' powered looms produced such wonderful fabrics that no one wanted the "old-fashioned" handmade things any more. The population was exploding westward; the frontier settlers welcomed the freedom to put their energy into necessities other than creation of cloth. Many aspects of the American economy had shifted from the home-based, self-sufficient, barter and trade, or small-merchant marketplace of a century before to an industry/consumer type of commerce. Men had left their looms to farm or seek gold or go into other businesses. Urban areas had mushroomed and employment outside the home became common. And the Civil War dealt the final blow. It cut established lines of supply for materials like cotton. It diverted financial resources into other channels. It drew men away from their farms and businesses to fight. When the battles were over and the pieces had settled the economy had been permanently altered.

There was a brief revival of coverlet weaving by some commercial mills at the time of the nation's centennial celebration in 1876. The coverlets woven

Between 1830 and 1850, Jacquard weaving became popular for coverlets. Jacquard looms allowed tremendous design freedom, but their use was limited to professional weavers who could afford them. Detailed information on this coverlet from the last quarter of the nineteenth century, which depicts deer, wild turkeys, and the Capitol building, can be found on page 189.

at that time are usually a poor-quality fabric with large central motif, loose weave, and garish colors, noticeably different from earlier pieces.

Hand-weaving of coverlets did linger on into the 20th century in a few places — through the work of an individual weaver or a religious colony here and there in New England or the Midwest, and through pockets of strong weaving activity in areas of the Appalachians.

The 20th-century revival of American hand-weaving began with a few individuals who rediscovered the old coverlets and the surviving weavers. These interested individuals saw a need to collect the woven pieces and knowledge still around before the coverlets were permanently destroyed and the information lost. They recorded or acquired coverlets and coverlet fragments, as well as written drafts, notebooks, and account books. They taught weaving and founded schools and donated their collections to museums. Today's weavers and historians and collectors owe a great deal to people like Laura Allen, Alan Eaton, Mary M. Atwater, Lucy Morgan, Edward Worst, Anna Ernberg, Lou Tate, and Marguerite Davison — these people saved coverlet weaving from complete extinction.

SMITHSONIAN INSTITUTION PHOTO No. 4358I-H

Pennsylvania weaver Peter Stauffer was born in 1791 and favored multi-shaft overshot patterns; as Jacquard weaving became popular his coverlet production dropped off, although he continued to make other types of cloth. One of his account books, shown at left, recorded some of his coverlet commissions from 1814. An excerpt from one of his pattern books and a partial coverlet are shown on page 47.

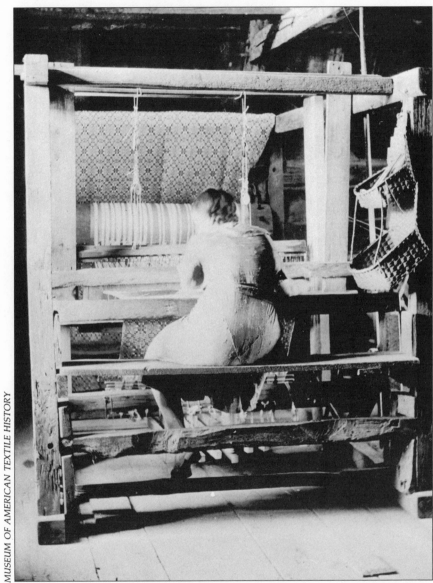

Four-shaft overshot coverlets were the province of home weavers, who produced two or three narrow panels and then joined them to get a fabric wide enough to cover a bed.

Who wove coverlets?

There were two main types of weaver: the home weaver and the professional. Some professionals worked from an established location and others took their trade on the road as itinerant craftsmen.

In early colonial America, most of the fabrics that were not imported were woven at home. Although not every household had a loom, most did have a spinning wheel or two. (Quite a few words and phrases have remained in our language from that time when creation of textiles was such a common part of everyday life that everyone understood the implicit meanings of the terms. Those were the days when a loom or a spinning wheel was important enough to be listed in a will, truly an *heirloom*. In some cases the occupation of a person became the person's surname; these names, too, have survived. You will find some terms of these types italicized in this book.)

Labor was usually divided among the family members. The men and boys did the work of raising the livestock and cultivating the crops (the *husbandry*). The girls performed such tasks as winding yarn on bobbins. If they remained unmarried as they grew older, they became the spinners (*spinsters*) of the family. For the most part, the married women were the *weavers* (*websters*, or creators of webs), although some men did get involved in the home-weaving. (Because it was mostly women who did the spinning and weaving, your maternal relatives are called the *distaff side* of your family, after the tool used to hold prepared flax fibers for spinning.)

A household that had no loom could still spin and dye, providing its own thread for a neighbor to weave. The labor was usually traded for something — in those days very little money changed hands.

Gradually this pattern of division of labor spread into the community as a whole. There were professionals who made a living by doing weaving for others (often, still, in exchange for food or a service). For a while some of the professional weavers were itinerants — they traveled around between remote communities. They did NOT, as one author has described it, "trudge about the countryside with their looms on their backs," for a Colonial-era loom was a large and heavy piece of furniture, definitely not portable! On occasion an itinerant might have disassembled his loom and hauled it from one place to another in a wagon. But apparently most traveling weavers moved on foot or horseback, arrived in a settlement, used whatever loom was available there, and exchanged skill and labor for room and board or for merchandise that could be traded or sold in the next community. There were probably relatively few itinerant weavers; like the Pony Express riders of a later time, they have been romanticized to a larger-than-life role in American history.

WHO WOVE COVERLETS?

All of the professional weavers of the 18th and early 19th centuries were men. In those days it was not socially acceptable for a woman to be in that kind of business *or* to travel alone and work outside her home. This attitude changed only slightly during the 19th century. As far as I can find, the only documented woman professional weaver was Sarah LaTourette, of Fountain County, Indiana. When her father died in 1849, she (age 27) and her brother (age 16) assumed their father's coverlet-weaving business and together operated it for several years. If you have a Jacquard-loomed coverlet with a woman's name woven in, the name is almost certainly that of the woman for whom it was woven, NOT that of the weaver.

Most of the professional weavers were men who were settled in one place. Many of them provided other related services, too. Some operated small carding and spinning mills. Sometimes a weaver was also a *dyer* who would dye wool or yarn to order. Sometimes he sold mill-spun yarn. Some weavers had finishing or "fulling" mills (which used *fuller's earth* in the processing of the woven cloth). A few also were skilled as *tailors* (or *taylors*) who would cut and fashion a garment from the finished cloth. Not all of the professional weavers operated alone; some had partners, apprentices, or employees, and some even operated small factories. On the other hand, not all of the professionals were full-time weavers — many were also farmers or operated other businesses.

Originally professional weaving began as part of the trend toward division of labor beyond the home. The man's loom was just like the home weaver's loom. But, being settled and having the financial or material support from his business, he could afford to invest in more shafts for his looms. He could also afford the money and space to have a wider loom (a *broadloom*), one which might have a fly-shuttle mechanism or require two people to operate, producing *broadcloth*. So when commercial mills began producing the everyday *(run-of-the-mill)* fabrics cheaply and in volume, he turned to weaving fancier fabrics and linens that could not yet be woven on mill equipment. Eventually, coverlets were a large portion of his product. When the Jacquard apparatus became available, it was the professional hand-weaver who could afford to buy it and install it, perhaps *raising the roof* or the ceiling of his weaving space to accommodate the towering attachment.

Although most professional weavers were men, Sarah LaTourette inherited her father's weaving business. This beautiful coverlet, shown in color on page 38 and described fully on page 191, was woven during the years when she and her brother were active.

GEORGE EASTMAN HOUSE

"Mrs. Sarah J. Wilson, Bulls Gap, Tennessee, 91 years old. In addition to daily work around the home, she finds time to raise some cotton, carding and spinning it herself. She also does some weaving. Oct. 22, 1933." This photograph was taken by Lewis Hine; another of his pictures appears on page 11.

Where were coverlets woven?

The answer to "where?" is closely related to the "when" and "who" of coverlet weaving. The home-weavers were the first. A coverlet woven by an individual on a household loom could have been made any time from 1760 to the present day, but most coverlets in the United States were woven between 1810 and 1850. A very early coverlet of this type is probably from New England or one of the mid-Atlantic colonies, the areas that were settled by that time. A mid-period coverlet is probably from the central eastern part of the nation (mainly New York, Pennsylvania, Kentucky, and Tennessee) or the South (where it might have been slave-woven). This reflects a population shift toward the southwest. A later 19th-century home-woven coverlet is probably from the Appalachian region, the only place where the craft lingered in any great strength. A 20th-century hand-woven coverlet could have come from anywhere! Since the 1920s there have been businesses and individuals making reproductions, especially in Kentucky and the New England region. And nowadays all hand-weavers, from Anchorage to Key West, have access to books that give pattern drafts and detailed information, as well as to appropriate yarns.

The early professional weavers seem to have worked mostly in Pennsylvania and surrounding states. Generally they did not work in urban areas, but in smaller towns central to large surrounding rural areas. The later professional weavers, especially the ones with Jacquard-controlled looms, worked mainly in Pennsylvania, Ohio, and Indiana. These areas were well settled by the 1840s and 1850s but were still remote from the east coast commercial textile mills and were therefore better markets.

There are overlaps of two or three decades in these periods of prime activity, but generally the century's westward expansion of population is reflected in the westward shift of the weaving regions. But by the time of massive emigration westward from the Mississippi River, hand-weaving was nearly dead. Coverlets were taken west in the wagons, but looms were not. Very, very few 19th-century American coverlets originated west of Illinois.

How were coverlets woven?

The answer to the question of "how?" has several parts including dimensions, fibers used, yarn preparation, dyes, looms and other tools, drafts, and finishes, all of which affect the result. Thousands of weavers with varying degrees of skill wove thousands of different coverlets on different looms with different hand-spun and mill-spun yarns. Even when a hand-weaver wove the same pattern twice she might have used different yarns or colors or a different width of warp. When a professional made two Jacquard coverlets on the same warp he might have woven them with different borders or even with entirely different center patterns. So there is no such thing as a "typical" coverlet. Nonetheless, we can make some helpful observations about coverlets in general.

Perhaps a more relevant initial question is, "How were coverlets different from other fabrics of their time?" The answer to that lies in a combination of loom availability and weave practicality.

In colonial and early independent America, most hand looms had either two or four shafts (called *leaves* in those days). The shafts are the loom's rectangular frames that rise or sink. I wind the warp yarns (lengthwise threads) of the fabric on a beam of the loom and thread them in a particular order through eyes of heddles on the various shafts. When I lower some shafts and raise others by pushing treadles, the threads on those shafts are lowered and raised, making an opening, or *shed*, through which I can place a *weft* (crosswise thread). If alternate warp threads are up and down so that the weft makes an over-one/under-one path, the fabric is called *plain weave* or *tabby*. If the weft makes an over-two/under-two path and if that path shifts by one warp thread to the side in each successive shed, making a diagonal line of skips, the fabric is called *twill*. A two-shaft loom produces only plain weave. A four-shaft loom can be used to make plain weave, twill, some weaves derived from twill (such as overshot), and other simple structures (such as huck, spot weave, and honeycomb). More complex weaves (such as satin, damask, doublefaced twill, and double weave) require looms with more than four shafts, looms which were not generally available to the early weavers.

Practicality is an important factor in the home-weaving of fabrics. For towels, curtaining, mattress ticking, sacking, rugs, and most other common household fabrics, as well as for clothing, we need the most efficient weave structure. That is usually plain weave, twill, or some very small all-over pattern like a *diaper* (diamond). These weaves are dense, firm, and balanced (so that neither the lengthwise warp threads nor the crosswise weft threads bear

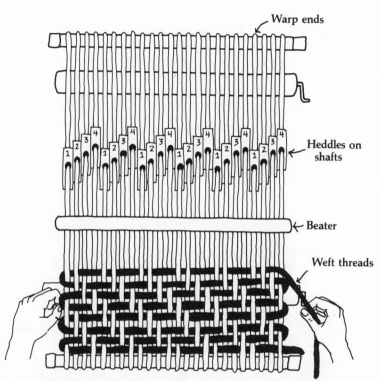

Warp ends

Heddles on shafts

Beater

Weft threads

Although a number of weave structures were used to make coverlets, plain weave and twill are the most basic weaving patterns. The loom above is threaded to a straight twill (successive warp threads go through heddles on shafts 1 through 4 in order, then repeat). The shafts determine which threads are raised for the weft to pass through, and therefore control the pattern. For the most recently woven weft thread, shafts 1 and 2 were raised. The beater is used to press the weft threads into place. It holds the reed which keeps the warp threads, or ends, in order.

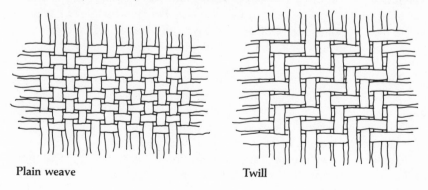

Plain weave   Twill

more of the wear). Because they require only one shuttle, they are faster to weave than a fabric which requires a second shuttle to carry the pattern yarn. They can be woven on the common two-shaft or four-shaft looms. Most patterning of these early home-woven household fabrics occurs through simple use of color: stripes, checks, or plaids. But a coverlet was woven for both decoration by day and warmth at night. It was not subject to as much wear as the other household fabrics were, so it could have a woven pattern with weft-skips. It was not worn on the body, so it could be a weighty fabric. The coverlet was the one piece of home-weaving that could use the more decorative patterning that was impractical in other pieces.

Fibers

Coverlets were made of linen and wool, cotton and wool, all cotton, or all wool. In the home-woven coverlets, the tabby weft (the thread which weaves the plain weave background) was usually single-ply or two-ply cotton, and the pattern weft that formed the design was almost always wool, a softer yarn somewhat larger in diameter than the cotton. Sometimes the wool was a single-ply yarn, highly twisted (to the point of kinkiness) to make it strong. When it was two- or three-ply wool, the individual plies were much finer, often very evenly spun, with considerably less twist (probably mill-produced). Before the advent of commerical spinning mills the fibers were grown and prepared at home.

Linen, which appears mostly in very early coverlets, is a bast fiber, the lengthwise inner bark fibers from the stem of the flax plant. Preparation of linen yarn is a long and laborious process involving *retting* (soaking), *braking* and *scutching* (beating and scraping), and other pounding and combing steps. The *heckle* (or *hackle* or *hatchel*) is a board with a block of long sharp nails that stick up in rows like a dog's raised hackles. Pulling a bundle of flax fibers across the nail points scrapes it free of "tow" (the short fibers) and combs it. (So, if you *heckle* me while I'm speaking, you are *needling* me with pointed remarks.)

Linen fibers that have been prepared this way are various shades of gray, cream, or tan (giving rise to the terms *flaxen-haired* and *tow-headed* for blond people). In Colonial times these natural colors of cloth were considered unattractive, so the linen fibers or woven cloths were usually bleached. In the 18th century, bleaching of linen involved steeping it in dung, *bucking* it in buttermilk, lye, ryemeal or bran, washing it, soaking it again, washing it again, and then *grassing* or *crofting* it (spreading it on the grass to be

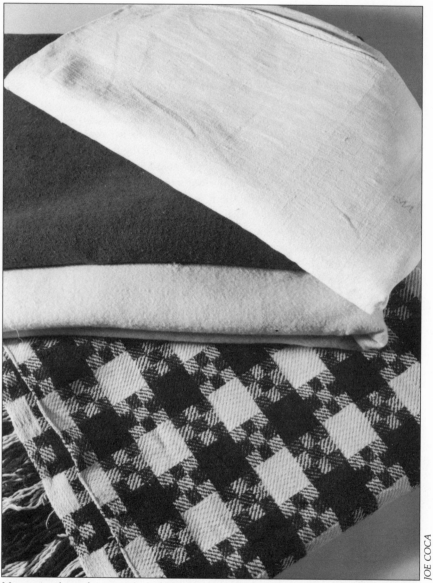

JOE COCA

Many simple and essential cloths were produced at home on two- and four-shaft looms. On top of this stack is a linen sheet; note the monogram. Below the sheet are two blankets, a white wool one (which has a blue stripe, not shown in this photo) and a deep blue one with a linen warp and wool weft. On the bottom is an apparently simple coverlet; its structure in fact requires sixteen shafts (details on pages 164–165). All of these fabrics appear in the color picture on page 40.

whitened by sun and rain). Linen is difficult to dye, so it was usually used in bleached or semi-bleached form.

The *line* linen fibers, between one and two feet long, were spun into fine strong thread used to weave sheets, mattress ticking, and other household fabrics, as well as for the background fabric of home-woven coverlets. The shorter tow fibers were spun and woven into coarser utilitarian fabrics such as *tow sacking*.

Not much cotton was hand-spun, but when machine-spun cotton thread became available it was so inexpensive and easy to get that most weavers promptly switched to using it instead of linen for their coverlets' warp and tabby. Most of the early mill-spun cotton thread was a fine single-ply yarn which the weaver could buy and ply double for warp strength.

Cotton is plant seed "hair," the fibers that grow from and surround a cotton seed in the boll. Processing these fibers (*lint*) involves separating them from the seeds and removing other debris, carding or fluffing them, and spinning. Cotton does not grow well in the northern American areas, and is harder than linen to spin on a wheel, so it was used very little in Colonial *homespun*. Instead, most of the early cotton fabrics were imported.

Originally cotton was bleached by the same methods as linen, since chlorine's bleaching effect was not discovered until the 1770s. The mercerization process, first discovered in the 1840s by John Mercer, is the treatment of cotton with caustic soda to make it stronger, shinier, and easier to dye. (Mercerized cotton threads are sometimes called *pearl* or *perle* cotton because of their pearly luster.) The mercerization process was not refined until the 1890s, so most coverlets are woven with unmercerized cotton, a dull off-white or cream thread.

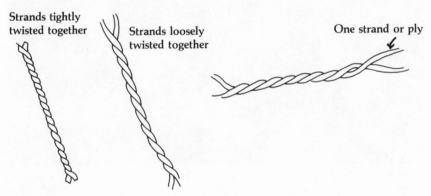

Strands tightly twisted together

Strands loosely twisted together

One strand or ply

Some yarns are single-ply, or composed of only one strand. Others, like these, are made of two (or more) strands twisted together.

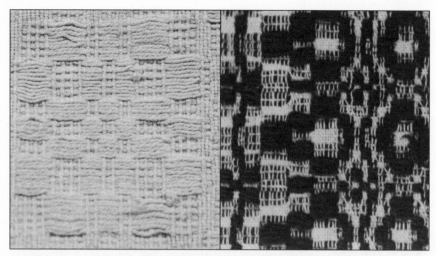

Left: *An all-white, all-cotton coverlet, with warp threads spaced at 18 per inch. (Details on pages 122–23.)* Right: *Made with cotton warp and ground weft and a wool pattern thread, this very fine coverlet has 58 warp ends per inch. (Details on pages 132–33.)*

Like linen, cotton is difficult to dye with natural dyes, so it was usually used bleached or unbleached. Occasionally I find a coverlet in which the cotton threads have been dyed a light blue, but that blue is usually very faded. All-cotton coverlets originated primarily in the hotter Southern states and are usually all white.

The finer the threads used in the warp, the closer together they can be spaced. Of the first hundred coverlets I documented, one had extremely fine warp threads and a warp count of 58 per inch. At the other end of the scale, only one had a warp count of fewer than 20 warp ends (threads) per inch — it was an all-cotton white coverlet at 18 e.p.i. (ends per inch). Most were the usual two-ply cotton at about 30 to 40 e.p.i.

Northern coverlets used wool in some role, either as supplementary pattern weft on the cotton (or linen) ground, or as warp and weft of the colored part of a double weave. Some double weave coverlets are all wool.

Wool is an animal fiber, the hair from sheep. The fleece (the entire coat of hair) is usually shorn from the animals in the spring, giving them the warm summer and fall months to grow a new protective coat. (Thus to *fleece* some-one is to take him for everything he has.) In the days when every bit of fiber was precious, women would even wander in the fields *woolgathering*, collect-ing tufts of wool that had caught on bushes and fences where the sheep had grazed.

Wool as it is cut from the sheep has quite a bit of natural oil (lanolin) coating the fibers. Sometimes wool is spun "in the grease" with the oil still on it. For this reason the spinning wheel was usually used near the fireplace in a Colonial home, where the warmth of the fire could soften the lanolin and make spinning easier.

Unlike linen and cotton, wool is easy to dye with natural dyestuffs if it is treated first with some kind of mordant (a metallic salt that will make the fibers accept the dye). It can even be dyed in fiber form, before spinning — if so treated, it is said to be *dyed-in-the-wool*, implying that it is the same color throughout every fiber of its being. It can also be yarn-dyed (dyed after spinning) or piece-dyed (dyed as woven cloth).

The warp and ground weft in this coverlet are made of a fine single-ply cotton, and the pattern weft is a single-ply wool. This is the coverlet's back; its front is shown in color on page 34 and a full description appears on pages 118–19.

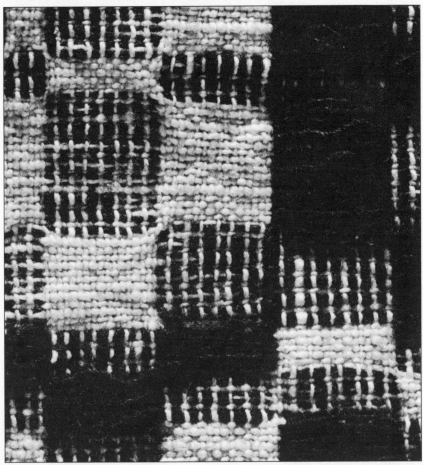

JOE COCA

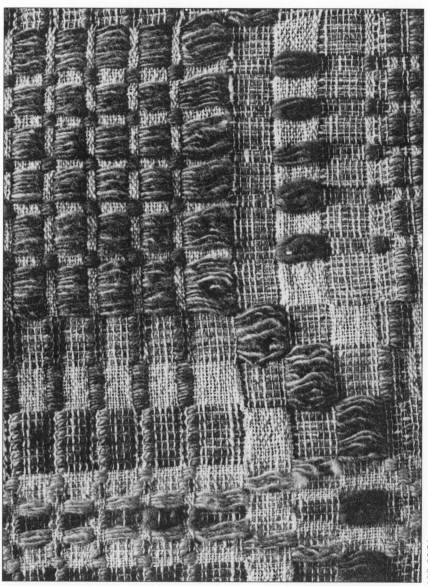

JOE COCA

This is the purple, green, and red coverlet shown in color on page 33. The warp and ground weft are single-ply cotton and the pattern weft is a single-ply wool, as in the coverlet on the opposite page. The dyes have faded unevenly. (Details are on pages 134–35.)

HOW WERE COVERLETS WOVEN?

Processing of wool includes cleaning it of debris and combing or carding it. (That usually meant using hand carders, sets of bent hook-like metal teeth mounted in leather on flat or curved wood boards with handles, to loosen and fluff the locks of fiber.) If wool is spun as a soft yarn with fibers going every-which-way, it's called a *woolen* yarn. If, instead, the fibers are combed so that they run lengthwise in the strand, making a finer, stronger, smoother yarn, the result is called a *worsted* yarn.

When the wool is from a white sheep, its natural color after washing or scouring (simmering in soapy water) is off-white. If this wool has been cleaned of all grease that would resist water, dyeing will give it a clear, uniform color. The mottled or heathered color that results from mixing in brown or gray or black fibers used to be considered undesirable. (So a *black sheep* was an outcast, excluded from the flock so that his strain of fleece color would not contaminate the purity and dyeability of the wool of subsequent generations.)

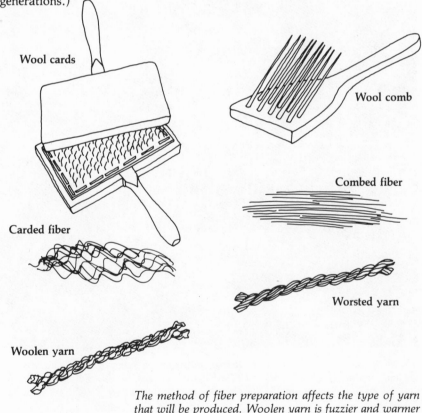

Wool cards

Wool comb

Combed fiber

Carded fiber

Worsted yarn

Woolen yarn

The method of fiber preparation affects the type of yarn that will be produced. Woolen yarn is fuzzier and warmer than worsted; worsted yarn is stronger and more durable.

A single pattern—in this case, Pine Bloom—can take on many appearances. The coverlet on the bed is a classic, blue-and-white version. The fragments show the effects of different weft colors. The folded coverlet is a threading variant with three colors in the weft. (More information on these coverlets can be found on pages 129–31 and 134—35.)

33

Cat Track & Snail Trail was a popular overshot pattern produced by home weavers. There are two major threading errors in this coverlet; one can be seen in the photo, in the second pair of "tracks" from the bottom. The upper pawprint is missing one of its edges. (See pages 30 and 118–19 for more on this coverlet.)

This Nine Stars & Table coverlet shows how the use of two colors can enhance a basic overshot design. The table is composed of large blue and small red blocks. The nine large blue stars are separated by small, two-step, red stars. (See also pages 51 and 114–15.)

35

The weave structure here is summer & winter. The blue coverlet is woven in a Wheel of Fortune (or Cup & Saucer) pattern, including both star and rose forms of a single motif. The red coverlet, shown also on the opposite page, is patterned with a single snowball surrounded by four roses and has a pine tree border. (See also pages 8, 80, 81, 158–59, and 162–63.)

Although the structures here differ, the motifs are the same. The center section of each coverlet is based on a snowball-and-ring combination and the border contains pine trees. The red coverlet is the summer & winter one shown opposite; the blue, white, and red one is a block double weave. (See also pages 8, 52, 162–63, and 174–75.)

JOE COCA

The date block in the corner of this coverlet is a trademark of Sarah and Henry LaTourette, who inherited their father's weaving business in 1849. This Jacquard pattern is called Frenchman's Fancy. The well-matched seam (at top of photo, running crosswise) and the use of color to highlight the motifs attest to the weavers' skill. (See also pages 20, 21, 54, and 191.)

This Jacquard coverlet contains a carnation and tulip medallion in its center, and is finished off with a rose border. Because of the lettering in the corner block, we can still tell that the cloth was woven by G. Nicklas, in Chambersburgh [sic], Franklin County, [Pennsylvania], probably in 1860. (See also pages 49, 52, 86, and 188.)

Although the "typical" coverlet may be a blue-and-white four-shaft overshot cloth, the actual diversity of colors and structures makes any use of the word "typical" suspect. All of the colors in the blankets, sheets, and coverlets shown here were available to coverlet weavers during the nineteenth century. (See also pages 9, 27, 120–21, 164–65, 172–73, 180–81, 184–85, 187.)

Dyes

Before the discovery of the first synthetic dye (a coal-tar derivative) in the 1850s, cloth was colored with natural dyes, which were extracts from plant and animal sources.

In coverlet-weaving times the most available, preferred dye was indigo, a strong dark blue extracted primarily from the *Indigofera tinctoria* bush. There were brief experiments in indigo-growing in some of the American colonies, but the product was of poor quality. Growers found that other crops were more lucrative, especially after a subsidy ceased at the outbreak of the Revolution. So most of the indigo used in America was imported, usually in the form of cakes of dried extract. Indigo is not water-soluble, and since the usual solvent used was "chamber lye" (fermented urine), the blue-pot was commonly simmered outdoors. A small piece of good indigo can dye a lot of wool, and the blue is colorfast, so indigo was widely used. By far the majority of American coverlets are blue and white (indigo-dyed wool and natural or bleached cotton).

The second most common early American imported dyestuff was madder, from the roots of a madder plant (usually *Rubia tinctorum*). The red from madder is commonly a brick or dark rust, but with the right treatment it is sometimes a bright red, the scarlet of "The *Redcoats* are coming!" (I have sometimes wondered if the American flag is red, white, and blue because madder-dyed, bleached, and indigo-dyed fabrics were what Betsy Ross happened to have in her scrap basket when the Founding Fathers came visiting.)

Several other vegetal dyes (mostly imported) were commercially available in early America. These include fustic and quercitron (yellow), logwood (black), and cutch (brown). According to one author, an alkali-soluble reddish dye from safflower colored the cotton *red tape* used to tie bundles of legal documents. The main imported animal dye was cochineal (pink-red), from tiny insect bodies.

For dyeing wool with most natural dyes the procedure is to boil the dyestuff in water to extract the color, then gently simmer the wool in the dye to the desired color. Almost any plant will yield at least some shade of yellow or tan when used to dye wool. So some early Americans used native plants to dye their yarns or fleece. Local vegetal dyes included butternut hulls and acorns (tan), unripe black-walnut hulls (the usual source of brown), various barks (browns and tans), smartweed, dock, goldenrod blossoms, and other barks or leaves (yellow), and alkanet roots and pokeberries (fading, or *fugitive*, reds). Overdyeing a yellow-dyed wool with indigo was done to get an olive or teal (never bright "Kelly" green). With the exception of quercitron, the native dyes were not cultivated on a commercial scale and so were not widely used.

Soon after the discovery in 1856 of the first synthetic dye, aniline violet (mauve), other dyes were synthesized. Many professional weavers used these new dyes, and late Jacquard coverlets often have bands of crimson, mauve, bright green, and mustard along with the classic indigo blue and madder red. Some of the early synthetic dyes were not colorfast, so the late coverlets are sometimes faded or mellowed to soft uneven hues except in the blue parts.

Equipment

The primary equipment used in the creation of a coverlet was, of course, the loom. A loom such as the coverlet weavers used is a large floor-standing piece of equipment, between five and eight feet in each dimension. Its functioning parts include the *warp beam* on which the warp threads are wound, the shed-opening mechanism, the *beater* holding the *reed* that keeps the threads evenly spaced and firms the wefts into place perpendicular to the warps, and the *cloth beam* on which the woven cloth is wound. Early American looms were so large and cumbersome that few have survived intact.

Many other smaller tools are used in textile work, and these still turn up in antique shops and attics and barn lofts. Most are tools for fiber processing and spinning; some are weaving equipment. Tools for linen preparation you might find include a flax brake, a scutching knife, a flax comb, or a hackle. For cotton and wool preparation there are the hand carders (that continued in use into the early 20th century for carding wool quilt batting). There are woolgathering baskets, sheep-shears, and dyepots. There are drop-spindles that a spinster used for making yarn without a wheel. And there are spinning wheels and yarn winders of various kinds.

Wool was usually spun on the tall *wool wheel* (also called *walking wheel* because the spinner stands and walks when using it, or *great wheel* because of the wheel's diameter, between four and five feet). The *flax wheel* is a smaller, low, treadled (foot-driven) spinning wheel at which the spinner sits to work. For linen spinning, the flax wheel has a distaff to hold the long prepared flax fibers in a smooth sheaf—some wheels also have place for a bowl of water with which to moisten fingers and fibers. The *Saxony wheel*, with its three legs and tilted table, is the most familiar type of small wheel, but there are other types, sometimes showing regional differences in shape and decoration. Flax wheels were not used exclusively for spinning linen—wool and cotton could be spun on them as well.

Flax brake

Hackle

Scutching tools

Wool wheel

Flax wheel

Niddy-noddy

Swift

Clock reel

43

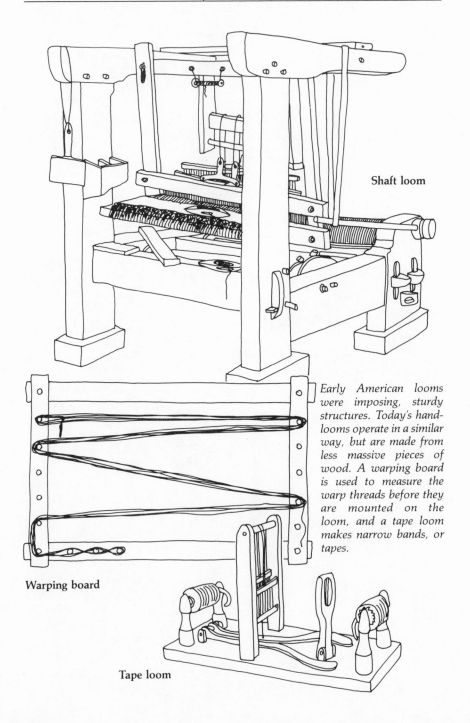

Shaft loom

Warping board

Tape loom

Early American looms were imposing, sturdy structures. Today's hand-looms operate in a similar way, but are made from less massive pieces of wood. A warping board is used to measure the warp threads before they are mounted on the loom, and a tape loom makes narrow bands, or tapes.

Devices for winding yarn were numerous. Some (such as the hand-held *niddy-noddy* or the floor-standing *clock-reel*) were used to reel yarn off the spinning wheel into skeins of standard length. Others (such as the table-clamped *swift*) were used to hold a skein while it was being wound off into a ball or onto a shuttle.

Some of the tools involved in coverlet weaving were used to make the yarn into warp for the loom. These include the *warping board* (a rectangular frame with pegs on which the threads are measured and put in order), the *raddle* (a bar with pegs that space the warp threads as they are wound onto the loom), and *leash-sticks* (a pair of smooth sticks that tie together and keep the threads in order as they are wound on).

Boat shuttle

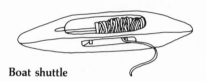

Rag or rug shuttle

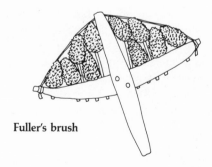

Fuller's brush

The *shuttle* is the tool that carries the weft back and forth through the open sheds of the warp when weaving (hence our modern *shuttle busses, Space Shuttle,* and *shuttle diplomacy* that involve going back and forth). There are different shapes of shuttles, many of which are used in modern versions today. (The fly-shuttles you now find in antique shops, the large heavy metal-tipped ones with wire brushes near the hole at one end, are usually old industrial equipment and not from hand-weavers.)

There are a few other pieces of small weaving-related equipment that you may see today in antique shops or museums. One is the *fuller's brush* (no relation to the famous door-to-door sales company). Such a brush consists of a braced Y-shaped handle supporting a row or two of dry teasel heads (from the plant *Dipsacus sativus*). It was used by the *fuller* (fabric finisher) to brush damp wool cloth to raise a nap or fuzzy surface. Such brushing and fulling was not usually done to coverlets, since wool and cotton shrink differently and such heavy processing would make a mixed-fiber coverlet pucker. But the tool was used on other fabrics contemporary to the coverlets, such as wool blankets.

Another tool that is sometimes found today is a *tape loom* for weaving narrow straps, tapes, and ribbons. It is a small box or frame, a few inches wide by a foot or two long, small enough to use in the lap or on a table. The tape loom was a valuable tool to have — in those days before dime stores and sewing machines and zippers, that's how the householder got seam binding, drawstrings, petticoat ties, ribbons, seed-sack ties, fringes, and innumerable other utilitarian and decorative tapes and ribbons needed to hold things together!

Drafts

A threading draft is the weaver's shorthand instructions for threading warp in a pattern on the shafts of the loom. It usually consisted of ruled horizontal lines representing the shafts of the loom. Numbers or marks written on or between the lines indicated the pattern threading, telling the weaver on which shaft each thread of the warp was to be threaded. Sometimes the draft also included cryptic notes concerning the pattern's name, the way the treadles should be tied to the shafts, and so forth. A draft was usually written on a narrow strip of paper which the weaver could stick with a pin to mark progress and could roll up and tie for compact storage. Paper was precious in the pre-industrial days, so every piece was used and reused. Drafts were sometimes written on scraps of paper, the backs of letters, the margins of advertisements, etc.

Some professional weavers did keep notebooks in which they wrote their drafts as well as their accounts. Such a notebook sometimes also included diagrams or *drawdowns* of what certain patterns would look like when woven — these could be used to show a customer the available designs. Since paper is even more perishable than fabric, few 19th-century paper drafts and weavers' notebooks have survived into the late 20th century — if you've found some in great-grandfather's dusty attic trunk, you've discovered treasure!

Opposite: *A star coverlet woven by Peter Stauffer, the Pennsylvania weaver shown on page 17. He took his pattern from an old German weaving book by Johann Michael Kirschbaum, dated 1771, which included patterns we are now familiar with under American names: Cat Track and Snail Trail, Whig Rose, Snowballs, and Stars. Below Stauffer's coverlet is the corresponding page in Kirschbaum's book.*

An historical draft format

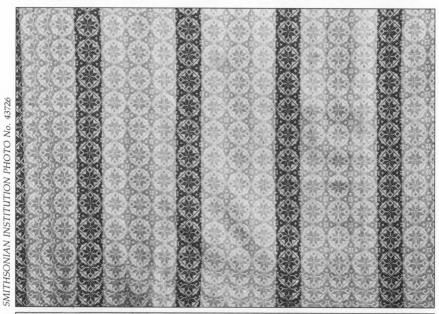

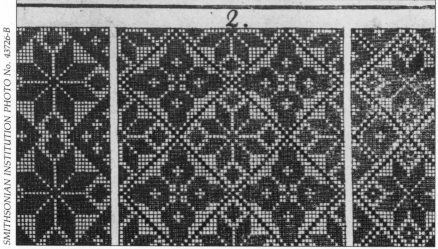

Dimensions

In the days of coverlet weaving, neither beds nor bedding (nor looms) were standard sizes—they were not mass-produced, so each piece was unique. Double beds were generally smaller than today's conventional sizes, but they were higher from the floor so there was plenty of room for decorative borders or parts of the coverlet pattern to show along the sides of the bed. The coverlet was tucked inside the foot of the bed (beds had solid footboards in those days), and occasionally you find a spread which has had its bottom corners cut away to accommodate the posts of a four-poster. At the head of the bed the coverlet was laid flat, with pillows atop it (sometimes covered by shams).

For most weavers, the maximum weaving width was (and still is) in the range of 36 to 45 inches—that's the widest the average person can reach comfortably to pass a weft-loaded shuttle from side to side through the open warp shed. So if the loom used a hand-thrown shuttle, the coverlet was woven in panels that were sewn together to make a wider bedcover.

Of the first hundred coverlets I documented, all were either two or three panels wide. The narrowest panels were 26 inches and the widest 40½ inches. The complete coverlets varied in width from 53 to 94½ inches—most were about 65 to 80 inches wide. In length they varied from 70 to 115 inches—most were about 80 to 95 inches long.

The *fly-shuttle* (or *flying shuttle*) mechanism made possible wider looms and cloth—sometimes over twice as wide. This device was invented in the 1730s (long before most of the other developments that enabled "production" weaving), but it wasn't widely used in the 19th century except by Jacquard weavers. There were a very few wide looms which did not use a fly-shuttle but were operated by two weavers as a team. If you have a seamless 19th-century coverlet, chances are it was woven by a professional man on a wide loom equipped with a fly-shuttle. (For an example, see the G. Nicklas coverlet opposite.)

Seamless coverlets come from very wide looms, usually owned by professionals. (Other photos of this coverlet appear on pages 39, 52, and 86, and a complete description is on page 188.)

Finishes

A weaver has several options for ways of sewing together the panels and finishing the edges of a coverlet.

Most of the 19th-century coverlets that were woven in panels were originally sewn together with selvedges (woven side edges) abutting, hand-stitched in an overcast or figure-eight stitch. Coverlets are generally heavy, and even heavier when wet, so a housewife who wanted to wash her coverlet would usually separate the panels to make them easier to launder. She might or might not have reassembled them in the original way. If the thread used to sew the seam of your coverlet is identical to a warp or weft, that's your tip-off to an original seam.

The normal finish for the top edge of a coverlet was a narrow hem, the cut edge of the fabric turned under twice about ¼ inch and hand-stitched.

This white, red, and green coverlet, woven in block double weave and shown in color on page 40, has a knotted warp fringe on its bottom edge. The edges which have been butted together and seamed are selvedges—the natural edges of the woven cloth. (See page 83 for another detail and pages 172–73 for more information.)

JOE COCA

This made a smooth firm edge that would lie flat under pillows by day and could be pulled around the sleeper's shoulders at night without tickling the face.

The side edges of most home-woven coverlets were usually the selvedges (the woven "self-edges" of the fabric where each weft thread reverses direction and turns around the edge warp thread). Professionally woven coverlets sometimes featured a pattern-weft fringe, with the cotton weft forming the selvedge and the wool weft extending as loops. Sometimes a coverlet has hemmed or bound edges, but those are usually a later modification, a mending of wear or damage.

The two commonest finishes for the foot of a coverlet were the narrow hem (same as the top) and the warp fringe (unwoven warp threads). Occasionally the end of the weaving was hand-stitched with whip stitch or hemstitching to prevent raveling. The fringe was infrequently knotted.

There are ways of making fringe separately, to be sewn to the edges of

JOE COCA

The back side of the coverlet shown in color on page 35 illustrates a seam which consumes some of the width of each panel. The panels' edges are selvedges and could have been butted and joined like the coverlet opposite; these panels may have been separated for laundering and rejoined as we see them. The bottom edges are narrow hems. Despite some damage in the hem areas, this coverlet is in fairly good condition. (Specific information is on pages 114–15.)

the coverlet. The easiest of these methods is to weave the fringe on the loom on the same warp as the coverlet. A loom-woven fringe can be quite elaborate, with narrow bands of pattern alternating with bands of openwork. When trim was made this way for a coverlet the bottom part was usually just woven as a continuation at the foot of each panel, and then additional installments were woven to be cut apart and hand-sewn to the sides of the coverlet.

The other primary way of making fringe for a coverlet was to weave it on a tape loom. For this, a narrow warp (of perhaps six to twenty threads) would be made using the same threads as the coverlet but very closely spaced in a warp ⅛- to ¼-inch wide on the tape loom. The wefts made fringe on one side of this. I have seen only one coverlet where tape-woven fringe had been stitched onto all four edges — usually only the sides and bottom end were decorated.

Opposite: *The top photograph shows an overshot coverlet with applied tape-woven fringe (details on pages 136–37). The middle photograph is of a structurally more complex coverlet with an applied tape-woven fringe; the fringe is separating from the coverlet due to wear (details on pages 184–85). The elaborate loom-woven fringe on the bottom coverlet consists of pattern bands, hemstitched areas, and leno twists (where warp threads cross each other in groups and are held in a twisted position by a weft thread). (This coverlet is described on pages 110–11.)*

The seamless Jacquard coverlet on the left (see also pages 39, 49, 86, and 188) has selvedges for its edge finishing. The five-block double weave coverlet on the right (see also pages 37 and 174–75) has warp fringe on the ends and selvedges on the sides.

JOE COCA

JOE COCA

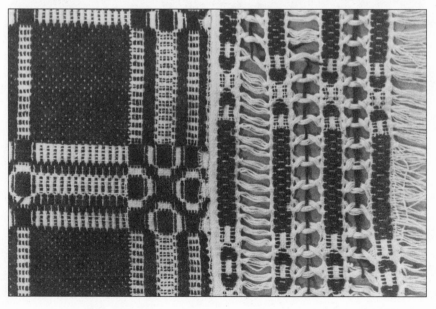

Pattern motifs

One of the first aspects of a coverlet to strike the viewer is its pattern. That pattern may appear very simple and rigid, or it may seem complex and vibrant. I know of one museum that even featured its coverlet collection as part of an exhibit on op art!

When a pattern is woven on a shaft loom it will, of necessity, be geometric. When it is woven on a Jacquard-equipped loom it can be very elaborate, realistic, and flowery, with finely defined curves.

The geometric pattern of a hand-woven coverlet is usually composed of one or more motifs — these motifs combine in myriad different ways to make different designs. Each motif or figure is made up of blocks of pattern (groups of threads that act together) that combine in a characteristic way. When you learn to recognize the motifs and how they are combined, you may find it easier to identify patterns.

The coverlet on the left has a geometric pattern and was woven on a shaft loom (see also pages 108–09). The one on the right, with its more fluid design, had to be produced with Jacquard equipment (see more of this piece on pages 21, 38, and 191).

COURTESY OF THE DENVER ART MUSEUM, DENVER, COLORADO

JOE COCA

The following motifs are geometric ones, woven on shaft-type looms.

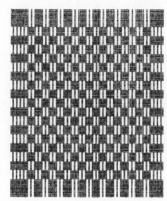

Table

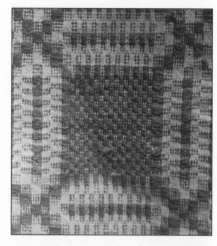

A **table** is a large square or rectangular motif formed by alternating two pattern blocks, as in a checkerboard.

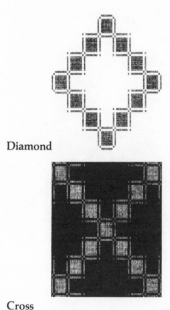

Diamond

Cross

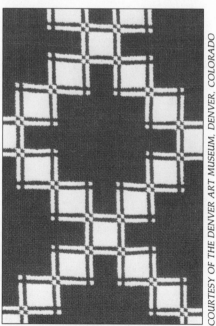

COURTESY OF THE DENVER ART MUSEUM, DENVER, COLORADO

Another simple figure is the **cross** (×) or **diamond.** It is formed by three or more blocks in a diagonal row that reverses, making a point.

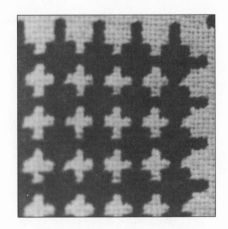

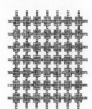

Slates

When the diamond is in three steps, and solid, it is called a **slate.**

Hammerheads

Several motifs are expansions of the cross or diamond figure. One is the **hammerhead** design.

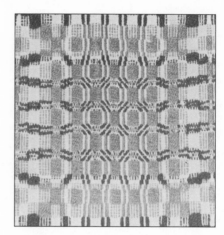

Garden

There is also the **garden** of diamonds enclosing single large blocks.

Sunrise

When the cross is extended it forms a radiating figure. If the size of each successive block increases as the diagonals get farther from the center, the motif is a **sunrise.**

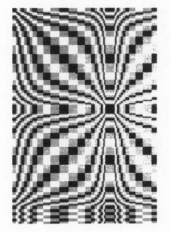 

Bowknot

If the size increases and then decreases as the diagonals extend, the figure is a **bowknot.**

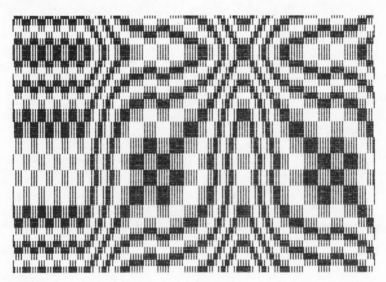

Blooming leaf

If the diagonal of the bowknot "stutters," it is a **blooming leaf.**

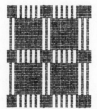

Star

A **star** is like a small table; it is made up of two blocks that alternate. When a star is woven in the conventional way so that its diagonals are connected and the motif has points, it is said to be **treadled star-fashion.**

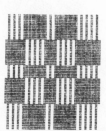

Rose (sometimes snowball or dogtrack)

When, instead, the inner parts are treadled first and the motif has a more rounded shape, it is said to be **treadled rose-fashion** and the resulting figure is called a **rose,** or sometimes a **snowball** or **dogtrack.**

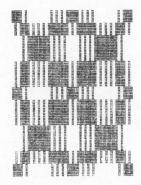

Small wheel

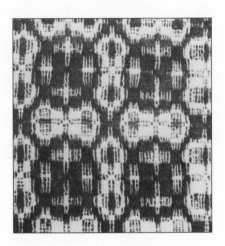

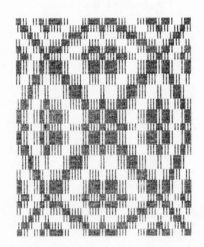

Large wheel

The **wheel** is one of the more complex woven motifs—it may be very small or large, but either way it appears to have a convex curved rim. A wheel is usually formed by a large center star, four smaller stars making "spokes", and a narrow repeat of the center making the rim.

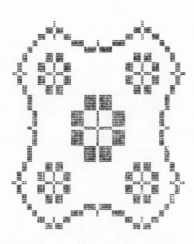

Wheel woven rose-fashions: five roses

When such a wheel is woven rose-fashion it forms a large rose and four small roses, all surrounded by an indented rim.

In some of the coverlet weave structures there are other motifs called stars—among them are the four-pointed **Star of Bethlehem** and the **eight-pointed star** familiar from European embroideries.

Star of Bethlehem

Eight-pointed star

There are also other motifs called **snowballs.** These are usually solid or open figures similar to the rose. When four are linked together horizontally and vertically the design is called a **double snowball.** Several fancy snowballs are so elaborate that they have their own names, including the Lisbon Star, the Sorrel Blossom, and the Virginia Beauty.

Snowball

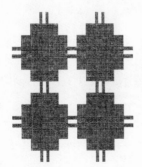

Double snowballs

The most familiar border motif is the **pine tree.** Since a border is an extension of the central motifs, there are many different tree forms, often with two or three "tree-trunks." Occasionally a coverlet even has double borders with two different "species" of trees!

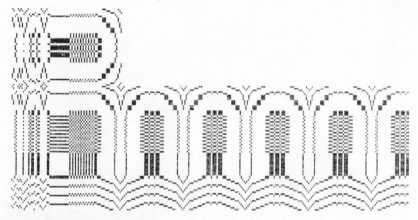

Pine tree border

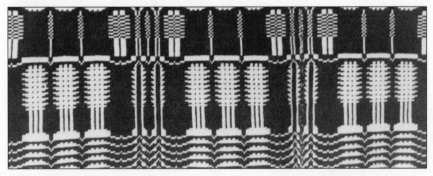

This unusually elaborate border consists of two rows of pine trees. (More information is on pages 176–77.)

Jacquard motifs

The patterns created on a Jacquard loom are quite different. A Jacquard pattern can be very detailed and realistic (well, at least realistic in a stylized way). So in a Jacquard pattern a **rose** will look like a flower, as will a **lily**, a **tulip**, or a **bluebell**. A Jacquard coverlet may show birds or animals (**eagle, rooster, distlefink, goldfinch, peacock, turkey, deer**) or even people (**hunter, farmer, George Washington**). It may have buildings (**cabin, courthouse, pagoda**) or vehicles (**train, sailboat**). There can be grapevines with grapes, urns full of flowers, birds' nests with baby birds, sixteen-point stars with floral centers, and an apparently infinite assortment of botanical representations. There seems no limit to what a Jacquard weaver could depict in his patterns.

The invention of the Jacquard mechanism provided nearly unlimited design potential. This floral Jacquard is described in detail on page 192.

Opposite: *The coverlet on top shows peacocks, flowers, and an Old Boston Town border. The bottom one has double roses in the center — compare these with the roses found in shaft-woven coverlets, as seen on page 59 — and a leaf-and-vine border. (More information on these coverlets is found on pages 190 and 186, respectively.)*

This page: *A number of motifs make up the center of this coverlet, which has trains in its border (see also page 193). It's easy to imagine the appeal of the sudden, unbridled freedom of design provided by the Jacquard loom. However, setting up a Jacquard loom to produce a particular pattern was time-intensive. Once the design was set and the cards punched to make it, a number of coverlets could — and would — be woven and sold. A full appreciation of Jacquard coverlets results in a renewed admiration for their shaft-woven predecessors.*

Pattern names

One entertaining aspect of coverlets is the names that the 19th-century weavers gave to their patterns.

Many of the names prosaically describe the motifs that compose the design — for example: Nine Stars and Table, Double Bowknot, Small Sunrise, Nine Roses and Table, Diamonds and Table, Sixteen Slates With Pine Tree Border, or Double Rose. There are some "more poetic" names in that category too — Open Window, Velvet Rose, Wreath Rose, and Double Chariot Wheel, for instance.

A large percentage of the patterns were named for a resemblance (real or fancied) to something in nature. There are Double Snowflake, Double Orange Peel, Cat Track & Snail Trail, Leopard Skin, Catalpa Flower, Cup & Saucer (Wheel of Fortune), many variations of Double Bowknot and Blooming Leaf (also called Maple Leaf, Oak Leaf, Double Muscadine Hulls, and several other names), and many, many others.

Often when a pattern was widely used it gathered several names. Perhaps the commonest of these popular multi-titled patterns was Pine Bloom (also called Pine Burr, Sea Star, The Seven Stars, Isle of Patmos, Sea Shell, Lady's Fancy, Pine Cone Bloom, and, in one variant form with stars, Gentleman's Fancy).

There are other patterns named Fancy — among them: Bachelor's, Young Man's, Dutchman's, Frenchman's, and Shuckeroon's. There are several Delights — Queen's Delight is one, and also King's, Ladies', Washington's, and Highlander's. There are patterns called Favorite, Choice, Felicity, Wonder, and Beauty.

A few of the pattern names hint at the homelands of immigrant weavers — as do King's Flower, King's Puzzle, English Flowers, Old Ireland, and Flowers of Edinburgh.

Patriotic, political, or historical titles include Whig Rose, Bonaparte's March, Indian Review, Federal Knot, Perry's Victory, Braddock's Defeat, Indian March, Indian War, Flag of Our Union, Freedom's Home, Old Glory, Harrison's March, and Mount Vernon. Such names might send *us* chasing to the history books to determine their significance, but to the weavers who named the patterns those were recent or contemporary events and thoughts.

Some of the pattern names mention states (which may or may not indicate the origin of the design). There are Kentucky and Virginia Snowball patterns. There are Alabama, Ohio, Connecticut, and North Carolina Beauty. Tennessee Trouble and Missouri Trouble are similar designs, and there's also

This coverlet pattern is called Freemason's Felicity, and is composed of a garden, four complete wheels, and a table. It is almost identical to Governor's Garden (which has fewer threads in each section and also goes by other names, including Mountain Cucumber and St. Ann's Robe). The photograph shows the back of this fragment. (See pages 142–45 for more details.)

Missouri Check and Missouri Compromise. Granite State is indirect, but Texas, Tennessee, North Carolina, Iowa, and Georgia all have their names in pattern titles.

Many patterns have Biblical or religious names. Methodist Wheel is another name for the Whig Rose design. I've already mentioned Isle of Patmos (Pine Bloom) and Star of Bethlehem. There are also Maltese Cross, Flowers of Canaan, Rose of Sharon, Walls of Jericho, Job's Trouble, Job's Perplexity, Star of the East, Crown of Diamonds, Morning Star, Christian Ring, and Fig Leaf (also called Barren Tree).

The pattern names we know about have usually come to us as oral tradition with a coverlet or as notations on written drafts. The origin of a name is

Tennessee Trouble consists of diamond-shaped double wheels, alternated with a divided table (see also pages 146–47).

hardly ever known, so we can only guess at when, why, and by whom a design was titled as it was. We can ask, as did the early 20th-century author Eliza Calvert Hall, whether Lee's Surrender was "named in sorrow or in triumph," but there is no sure answer. We can speculate whether the New England sea trade with the Orient influenced the designing and naming of the popular Jacquard border known as Boston Town (with pagodas and palm trees among the churches and courthouses). But we can only speculate. If the relationship of a pattern to its name is not evident, we can only wonder about it, as we do about the design called Guess Me!

Lee's Surrender is a pattern of repeated stars, separated by tiny, two-step crosses, surrounded by an elaborate border with a sunrise and four tables. (See also pages 154–155).

Weave structures

In a fabric, the structure of the weaving (the way the threads interlace) has a lot to do with the appearance and characteristics of the fabric. Along with fiber content, color, and pattern, weave structure is an important element in a coverlet's identity. Many different weaves were used for coverlets; for economy of space in this book I have grouped them into the following categories, roughly in order by increasing complexity:

- Plain weave, twill, and other two-shaft and simple four-shaft weaves
- Overshot weave
- Summer & winter weave
- Doublefaced twill block weave
- Block double weave
- Other multi-shaft weaves
- Jacquard single weave
- Jacquard double and tied doublecloth weaves

Even for a non-weaver, an understanding of the basics of these weave structures can help in coverlet identification.

This two-shaft weft-faced fragment came from a two-panel coverlet woven with a cotton warp; the light weft is also cotton, and the dark weft is wool. All are very fine single-ply yarns (see also pages 100–01).

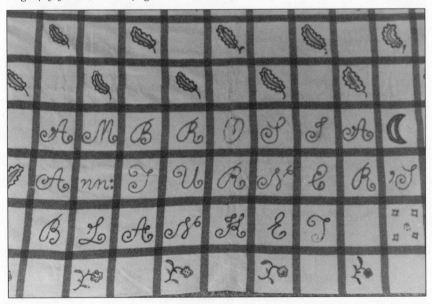

Plain weave, twill, and other simple weaves

As described earlier in this book, *plain weave* and *twill* are the simplest weaves used in early American bedding. Because these structures make dense but relatively thin unpatterned cloth, they were used for sheets (usually linen) and blankets (usually wool). Such a fabric's only decoration might be vertical stripes or horizontal bands or checks or plaids of color. Examples of several simple fabrics appear in the photographs. On page 27, the photo shows a plain weave linen sheet, a plain weave white wool blanket with bands of blue, and a dark blue "linsey-woolsey" blanket (linen warp, wool weft). The photo on page 40 of the color section includes a brown plaid twill blanket. On page 9 is a tied quilt which has a white wool blanket backing, carded wool filler, and a pieced top of assorted hand-woven plain weave and twill clothing and blanket fabrics.

Plain weave and twill bedding could also be embellished with embroidery. The needlework might be as simple as cross-stitched initials in a corner to identify and number the piece, or it might be as elaborate as a crewelwork sampler.

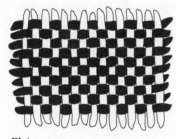

Plain weave

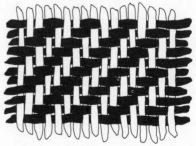

Twill

HOW WERE COVERLETS WOVEN?

There is a *two-shaft weft-faced* coverlet weave that appears rarely. (Weft-faced means that the weft threads are packed in so that they completely cover the warp threads.) In this weave, two colors of pattern weft alternate to form opposite-color thick and thin columns. The warp is usually cotton or linen, and the wefts are normally blue and white wool. Because this weave needs only two shafts on the loom, it could have been used by any weaver, but it was apparently not widely known.

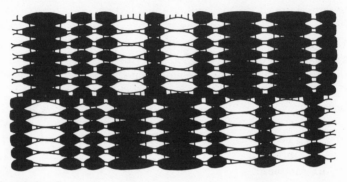

Two-shaft weft-faced

There are a few other four-shaft weave structures that were occasionally used for coverlets (not shown here). One is *honeycomb*, in which tiny "cells" of fine plain weave are outlined by heavier threads. The honeycomb coverlets I have seen have been all white, woven of fine bleached cotton.

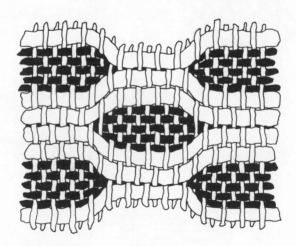

Honeycomb

This two-shaft weft-faced fragment came from a two-panel coverlet woven with a cotton warp; the light weft is also cotton, and the dark weft is wool. All are very fine single-ply yarns.

Another weave possible with four shafts is *M's & O's* (name origin undetermined). In this structure there is just one weft, which weaves alternate areas of plain weave and corded columns. The weave was used primarily for household linens, but I have seen one M's & O's coverlet — it had white wool warps and dark blue wool wefts.

M's & O's

A third little-used four-shaft weave is *undulating twill.* This is a twill threaded in such a way that some warp threads are doubled, tripled, or quadrupled, making the diagonal line of the twill widen and narrow so it appears to undulate. The one coverlet I have seen in undulating twill had a natural cotton ground with red and brown pattern wefts.

Undulating twill

Opposite: *Overshot offers a tremendous number of design possibilities; nearly all home-woven coverlets were produced in this structure. This coverlet is Cloudless Beauty (see also pages 104–05), a "Patch"-type pattern composed primarily of two blocks.*

Overshot weave

By far the most common weave used in coverlets, the weave used for virtually all the home-woven coverlets, was *overshot*. The name comes from the structure, which is a plain weave ground with pattern wefts "overshooting" and "undershooting" the ground fabric in variable blocks of skips. Patterns in overshot weave are repetitive geometric designs that sometimes have borders along the sides and across the foot of the coverlet. On a four-shaft loom, the variety of geometric patterns possible with just four blocks is tremendous. The designs range from the cleanly defined "Patch"-type patterns

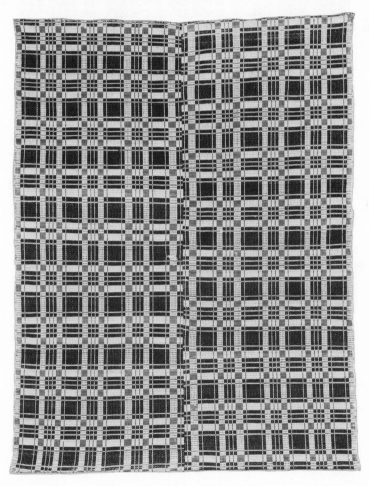

like Cloudless Beauty to the extremely elaborate ones like the border of the Lover's Knot On Opposites.

An overshot fabric usually has three textures: the blocks of pattern weft skips, flanking columns of *incidentals* where the pattern weft weaves plain weave alongside the ground weft, and blocks of plain ground where the pattern wefts "undershoot."

In ordinary overshot, the yarns are usually dark blue or brick red wool pattern on an unbleached cotton warp and ground weft. But sometimes the ground is light blue, and the pattern is often brown, mustard, blue-green, pink, black, or another natural-dyed hue. Illustrations of overshot coverlets are scattered throughout this book.

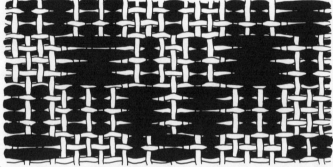

Overshot

Overshot on opposite blocks has the same characteristics as the regular weave, but it looks different because the blocks of overshots and pure background areas are adjacent to each other and the two sets of incidentals are mixed, giving the pattern a very grayed look. This variation of the weave is uncommon; it is usually woven with a blue wool pattern yarn and unbleached cotton warp and tabby threads.

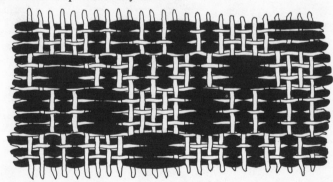

Overshot on opposite blocks

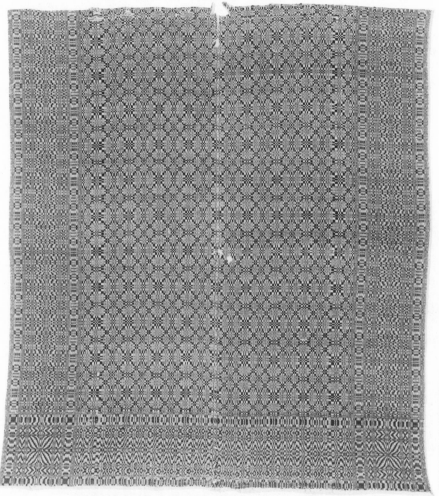

At the opposite end of complexity from Cloudless Beauty is this Lover's Knot on Opposite Blocks, with an extremely elaborate border. (More information is on pages 126–28.)

Summer & winter weave

Summer & winter weave has a plain weave ground fabric with pattern weft yarns interlacing it in an over-three/under-one path. A common four-block design that could be woven on four shafts in overshot requires six shafts in summer & winter. This means that it was beyond the capabilities of virtually all the early American home weavers.

The weave requires two shafts for the tie-down threads that alternate, securing the pattern wefts to the plain weave background, plus one shaft for each block of the pattern. Summer & winter patterns are commonly four-block designs and occasionally have borders. There seem to be fewer coverlets in summer & winter than in some of the other professionally used weaves.

As in all other shaft-loom weaves, patterns in summer & winter are geometric. They have only two textures: predominantly pattern and predominantly background. Because the usual yarns for this weave were unbleached cotton warp and tabby weft with dark blue wool pattern weft, and the pattern and background are normally unequal in area, the appearance is usually dark on one face and light on the other face of the coverlet. This has given rise to the popular misconception that "if your coverlet is dark on one side and light on the other, it's summer & winter." Actually, *most* coverlets have a darker and a lighter face. The distinguishing feature in summer & winter is that the tie-down skips of successive pattern threads or pairs overlap alternately, like bricks. If the pattern is geometric, with blocks formed of three-thread skips in a brick-like pattern, you are looking at summer & winter.

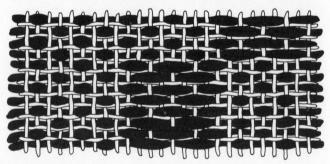

Summer & winter

Opposite: *At left is an example of summer & winter (shown also on pages 8, 36, 37, and 61; this coverlet described on pages 162–63). On the right is the doublefaced twill coverlet also seen on pages 27 and 40 (details on pages 164–65).*

Doublefaced twill block weave

Doublefaced twill block weave (also called *double twill* or *twill diaper*) is a structure which has no plain weave ground. Instead, the warp and pattern-weft threads interlace directly in blocks that are weft-dominant twill on one face and warp-dominant twill on the other. In this weave each block of pattern requires four shafts of the loom, so a typical four-block pattern needs a sixteen-shaft loom, as only the professional weavers had.

Doublefaced twill coverlets are either cotton and wool or all wool. The example included in the collection on page 27 is blue wool and white cotton in unusual checks that change the appearance of the structural pattern.

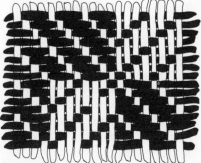

Doublefaced twill block weave

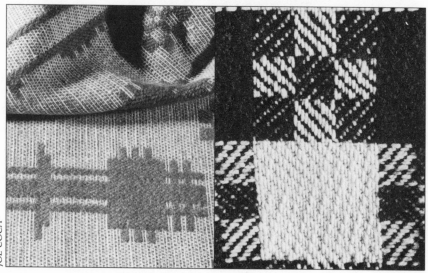

JOE COCA

Block double weave

In *double weave*, two complete sets of warp and weft are used; each set interlaces with its own wefts in a plain weave fabric. The two layers weave simultaneously. The pattern is formed by the interchange of the two fabrics between layers.

In block (shaft-controlled) double weave, each block of pattern requires four shafts of the loom, so a four-block pattern needs a sixteen-shaft loom. Patterns range from three-block to seven-block; four- and five-block designs are commonest. Double weave was apparently the most-used of the professionals' weaves. The geometric patterns are bold and often have borders at the foot and sides—this weave is the one where most pine tree borders occur.

The yarns used for double weave are most often dark blue wool warp and weft for one layer and either white cotton alone or a combination of white cotton and red wool for the other layer. Many other combinations are possible. I have seen double weave coverlets with the cotton layer partly light blue, with the red and blue wools on one layer and the white cotton on the other, with both layers all wool, and with the wools other colors (although this last is uncommon). The block double weave coverlet in the collection on page 40 (also opposite left) is unusual, with red and green wool and white cotton layers.

Block double weave

Other multi-shaft weaves

In modern weavers' parlance, *multi-shaft* means a loom with more than four shafts. (The shafts are usually in multiples of four, hence the "multi-.") There are a variety of less frequently used coverlet weaves that can be included in this category, although I don't have room here to go into the fine points of their classification. These multi-shaft weaves include various point twills, like the blue and coral and olive wool fragment in the collection on page 40. They also include an assortment of different structures that weave Star & Diamond patterns, like the fragment and the Tulips and Roses coverlet in the collection on page 40. Some of these weaves resemble overshot, since they have blocks of weft skips on a plain weave ground, but they have many more than overshot's usual four blocks in their patterns. In some ways they are like summer & winter, since they have regular tie-downs which anchor the weft skips, but the skips vary in size and are in blocks instead of singles or pairs.

Shafts required for these different weaves vary from eight to twenty-four, so virtually all of them were the products of professional weavers.

On the left below is the block double weave coverlet which also appears on pages 40 and 50 (details on pages 172–73). On the right is an eighteen-shaft Star & Diamond pattern (details on pages 182–83).

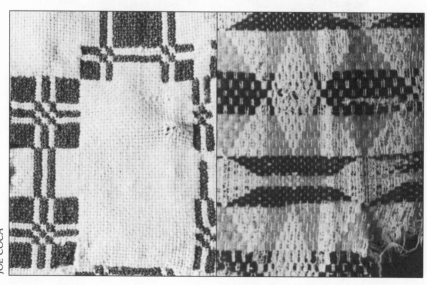

JOE COCA

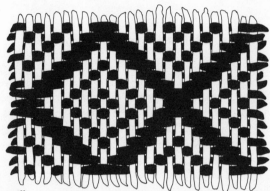

Nine-shaft point twill

Three-block ten-shaft point twill

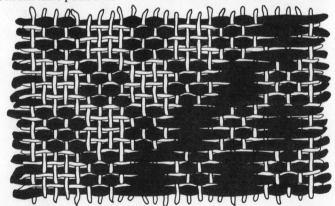

Sixteen-shaft repeat twill

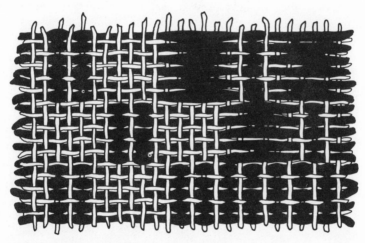

Eighteen-shaft two-tie unit weave

Jacquard weaves

All of the above weave structures are shaft-loom weaves and their patterns are geometric, limited by the number of shafts. But having a Jacquard mechanism with a 315-hook head and cards is like having a 315-shaft loom. Tiny steps of a line and gradations of a curve are possible in a Jacquard pattern, regardless of the weave structure used.

A Jacquard-woven coverlet usually has a border, and often a special corner where the borders meet at the foot. This corner may include a trademark — see *A Checklist of American Coverlet Weavers* for a guide to these. Or it may contain one or more pieces of information, such as the name of the weaver, the name of the customer, the place (city, county, township, state) or the year of manufacture. Very occasionally a coverlet includes all of these.

The weave I call *Jacquard single* is really a family of similar weaves. All use a single set of warp threads; certain threads at regular intervals (every third, fifth, sixth, or eighth warp end) are *tie-downs* which anchor the pattern wefts to the plain weave ground. The structure is similar to that of summer & winter, and Jacquard single coverlets are sometimes thus mislabeled. A summer & winter design is always geometric because it is shaft-controlled, whereas a Jacquard design is ornate and flowery because it is controlled by punchcards. Summer & winter never has weft skips longer than three threads, whereas in the Jacquard the skip lengths depend on the structure used.

You will usually find a Jacquard single weave coverlet has been made with a wool pattern weft on a ground of cotton warp and weft. The warp is usually white or natural; sometimes the tie-down warp threads are pale blue or, occasionally, gray or light brown. (All of the coverlets I've seen with colored tie-downs have been from Pennsylvania, Indiana, or Ohio — mostly the latter.) The pattern colors may be the usual dark blue and dark red, but they are equally likely to include additional broad bands of mustard, green, rose, and dark turquoise. The example in the collection on page 40 (also at left below) is an unusually stylized pattern of strawberries in the unusual color combination of red and olive green.

Approximation of a **Jacquard single;** *these are the pattern threads and there are also tabbies, or ground weft, in the complete structure.*

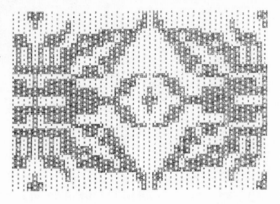

86

Like the block double weave, *Jacquard double weave* has two sets of warps which interlace with their own wefts, forming two separate plain weave cloths that make a pattern by intersecting. The primary difference is that the block double weave, being shaft-woven, is geometric, whereas the other, being Jacquard-woven, is ornate and flowery.

A Jacquard double weave coverlet usually consists of a cotton warp and weft on one layer and an all-wool warp and weft on the other, although some were woven of all wool. Very late Jacquard doubles usually have a cotton warp for both layers.

The common blue-wool and white-cotton color scheme prevails in this weave, too, but some weavers used broad stripes and bands of other colors of wool. As with the other weaves, the use of aniline or synthetic dyes indicates a later (post-1850s) date.

Once in a while you will find a coverlet that is a hybrid of the two Jacquard weave types. It will have pattern areas that are typically single, with tie-downs anchoring the pattern wefts, and other areas that are double, with two separate layers of plain weave fabric. One author calls this *tied doublecloth.*

Opposite: *On the left, a motif from a Jacquard single coverlet (see also pages 40, 90, and 187). On the right, a motif from a coverlet in Jacquard tied doublecloth (see also pages 49, 52, and 188).*

Dicie Fletcher, who appeared on page 11, is shown in the late 1800s, winding handspun yarn from a skeiner into quills for weaving. Her coverlets were woven with between 40 and 48 warp threads in each inch.

Handling a coverlet

What to look at in a coverlet

Certain details will help you identify and/or evaluate a coverlet, whether you own the piece or are seeing it in a dealer's shop or a museum. (If the fabric is in a museum, remember that the primary purpose of that location is its preservation. The oils on your skin can cause fabric to deteriorate more quickly—"Look with your eyes, not with your hands!")

Look at the **weave structure** of the coverlet—this will tell you a lot about its provenance and rarity. You can deduce such things as the type of weaver and loom: overshot on four shafts (therefore a woman at home?), summer & winter or other multi-shaft weave (therefore a professional man?), Jacquard (therefore a man—or Sarah LaTourette?). If the weave is overshot or block double weave or one of the Jacquard structures, you'll know you have a better chance of documenting the pattern, simply because more coverlets of those types survive and therefore have been described in print. On the other hand, if the weave is an unusual or less frequently used one, you'll know the piece might have a higher value because of its relative rarity. If you can determine the **pattern name** in addition to the weave, so much the better.

What **fibers** and **colors** were used in the coverlet? Determining these elements could help you date the piece, at least roughly. For instance, if it's an overshot that is really linen and handspun wool, it's probably very early (pre-1810). On the other hand, if it's Jacquard double weave with cotton warp in both layers and synthetically dyed wool weft in one layer, you'll know it's a very late piece (probably post-1870).

What are the coverlet's **dimensions**? Is it **seamless**? If it has seams, how many are there and are they well matched? If the coverlet is only a fragment, does it have any signs of selvedges or seams? Are there threading or treadling **errors** in the weaving? These things will help you determine the weaver's skill level and the quality of the original weaving job. For example, major threading and treadling errors in an overshot, or a very poorly matched seam, could indicate an inexperienced weaver. If the dye colors in the wool are strong but very uneven, or if there's a noticeable color change (such as six inches of blue weft at the end of one panel of an otherwise green coverlet), that could indicate an amateur dyer (or a poor planner). In a Jacquard coverlet, scattered dots or single flawed lines that show up the same in every repeat of the pattern probably mean that the weaver was using a set of punched cards so worn that unplanned holes had developed from the pressure of the rods. Conversely, a strong, well-woven coverlet with solid colors, matched seams, and no flaws indicates a good weaver.

What **edge treatments** were used on the coverlet? Are the ends the usual narrow hems? Are the sides selvedges? If the coverlet is double weave, how are the selvedges woven — as separate layers, or with both wefts circling a common warp thread, or with wefts interlocking? Are there fringes? If so, are they warp fringes, weft fringes (which wefts?), or added loom-woven or tape-woven or twined fringes? Professional touches, such as well-made trim, can contribute to the overall value of a piece, even if it's only a fragment.

Does the coverlet have any **identifying marks**? An occasional home-woven coverlet may have embroidered or woven-in initials (and possibly a date). A professionally woven shaft-weave coverlet will sometimes have a similar embroidered identification. A Jacquard coverlet is more likely to have its identification woven into the lower corners or borders.

If you own (or are thinking of buying) the coverlet, an important aspect to determine is its **condition.** Is it whole? Is it still firm? (Holding it up with light behind it will show up worn areas or small rips that might not be obvious otherwise.) Is each seam still intact? How badly worn or torn are the top

Signature blocks can appear in both Jacquard-woven coverlets (left) and shaft-woven coverlets (right). (The lefthand coverlet also appears on pages 40, 87, and 187; the righthand coverlet is the very old one from the Winterthur collection, seen on page 13.)

JOE COCA

COURTESY, THE HENRY FRANCIS DU PONT WINTERTHUR MUSEUM

(where it was tugged around shoulders), the selvedges (where it was rubbed against), and fringes, if any? Wear seldom occurs along the center sides — the old beds were higher from the floor than modern ones (and perhaps mothers were stricter), so the coverlets were not strained by being sat upon! Look for moth damage in the wool areas (moths eat only animal fiber) and for wear damage in the cotton areas. If threads or pattern areas are damaged, try to determine if the cause was internal (such as from abrasion of harsh threads, or from acid dyes) or external (such as from strain or sun-rot). Are there stains? Have the cotton threads yellowed or the colors faded? If so, try to determine if the color changes are throughout the piece (indicating a problem with the original dye or fiber) or localized to one face or one area (indicating undue exposure to light or another textile enemy while on a bed or folded). Inspect the piece for signs that it has been put to some other use (such as curtain headings or rusty curtain-ring marks). Generally, are there any **outstanding features** or **conditions** of this piece that might increase or deflate its value?

Finally (and very importantly), determine what you can of the coverlet's **history,** and write down that information to put with the piece. Possibly you only know that your piece was bought from an antique dealer in Wobegonville, Ohio, in 1972 or '73. Well, at least write that. Or perhaps you know that the family legend has been that "Grandma Matilda Whistler Bexendorfer (who was born in Remote Station, Wyoming, in 1864) spun and wove it." Write that down, even though the coverlet is a signed Jacquard by a Pennsylvania man in 1846. Label the information about Grandma Matilda as myth, and then do a little digging into your family's genealogy. You might find that her mother was Bertha Grumblefinger Whistler, who was married in 1844 in a county of Pennsylvania near the weaver. If so, you have good cause to believe that the coverlet originally belonged to Matilda's mother and was handed down. Whatever you find out, write it down. If you find out nothing, write down where you've searched (so that another generation of interested owners won't have to retrace your futile steps). Or maybe you know exactly who wove the coverlet and have two shuttles, an account book, three wills in which the coverlet is itemized, and an old daguerreotype of the coverlet's first owner to prove it. Ah, blessed are you among coverlet owners! Please write down the information, make photocopies of the documents and pictures, put the copies in a file envelope with the coverlet, put the originals in your safe-deposit box, and bask in the knowledge that you are highly unusual!

How to care for a coverlet

The very rare surviving ancient textiles have all been found in dark, cool, dry places — undisturbed caves in regions where annual precipitation is measured in fractions of an inch. This tells us something about the preservation and the destruction of cloth.

Any textile has several enemies, mostly unseen ones. The main ones are wear, acid, light, humidity, and insects.

In the case of a coverlet, *wear* might include abrasion by dirt particles or handling or use, tearing from the strain of being sat upon, staining from body oils, or even breakage just from being shaken or hung to air. I've had a coverlet start to rip from its own weight when it was folded and hung in a storage closet (before I knew better). The abrasion could be inherent in the coverlet — if one of the yarns used is harsher, coarser, or disproportionately stronger than another, the weaker yarn will give way. There isn't much you can do about that particular problem except protect the cloth from strain. But sometimes you can clean a coverlet, and you can always avoid handling it or doing other damaging things to it.

Acid is a hidden textile enemy that can come from many sources — from the paper in which your coverlet is wrapped, from the wooden shelf or chest on which it lies, even from cigarette or cigar or pipe smoke. Such smoke may be the worst of these — it permeates the cloth, and when it combines with the air's humidity it becomes an acid that gnaws at and weakens the fibers. Acid, too, may be inherent in the cloth if a dye or a laundering agent used in its manufacture or care has been too acidic.

Light may be the least recognized enemy of a textile. We realize that prolonged exposure to direct sunlight can make colors fade, but we forget that the same exposure can destroy the fibers themselves. My personal lesson in this was learned when I had to replace our strong, dense, modern living-room carpeting — the untouched segment between the curtain and the south floor-to-ceiling window was worn completely away (pile, backing, and all), simply from sitting for fifteen years in the sun. Even relatively dim indirect light, if unfiltered, has this effect, although the damage happens more slowly and over a longer period of time. Big museums, which are in the business of preserving things for centuries, strive for dim, carefully controlled, and filtered lighting. They usually won't permit you to take flash pictures, since one instantaneous intense flash could be equivalent to months of conservative light.

High *humidity* and enclosure in an *air-tight container* are also destructive to textiles. Mildew growth, encouraged by moisture, can cause permanent stains on the cloth. Too little humidity is also potentially harmful if the textile is going to be moved or folded — fibers which are continually subjected to dry heat will become brittle and easily broken.

So the "worst-case scenario" for care of your coverlet would be to dry-clean the coverlet in a self-service machine and overheated dryer, then tear it into five pieces. You would use two to line the south window curtains, one to protect your wooden table from a rough pottery lamp and from beverage-glass sweat, and one to upholster your heavyweight cigar-smoker's favorite chair. The fifth piece you would make into toss pillows, and the scraps into little, tightly stuffed animals to be nailed to the wall. You would arrange the chair, table, and pillows in a cozy grouping around your fireplace, where the dry heat and ambient fumes could complete the destruction that the dry-cleaning, heat, tearing, sewing, soaking, strain, light, and smoke had begun.

Or, in your innocence, you could donate the coverlet to your untutored, volunteer-run local museum. They would love to have it, and would fold it neatly (so only a three-inch strip of it could be seen), and stack it atop other fabrics in a closed, fluorescent-lighted, glass showcase which originally held candy and food in the town's first general store. They might honor your donation by labeling the piece with your name and the year you gave it (the label being on a pronged metal butcher's price marker which is jabbed into the coverlet and will soon rust in your humid climate). When the museum receives yet another coverlet you won't know whether to hope or to fear that it will be stacked atop yours (hope that it will protect yours from that hot

JOE COCA

unfiltered fluorescent bulb, or fear that its weight will increase the strain on the folds of yours).

But those are both "horror stories," the worst of the worst. You won't do either of the above because your coverlet is a family heirloom which you love and want to preserve. So what's the "best-case scenario"? Well, of course, if the coverlet is in mint condition the very best thing for its long-term survival would be donation to a big professional museum which would use conservation laboratory methods to clean, store, and display it.

This poor overshot coverlet has been badly treated.

Or you could get involved in that local museum as a volunteer or board member, donating money to sponsor conservation seminars and finance proper storage and display facilities.

But if you want to keep and appreciate your coverlet yourself, there are some things you can do to slow or halt further deterioration.

You can clean the coverlet (very carefully, by hand). To do so, spread the coverlet flat in a clean dry place. Vacuum it gently, using a hand vacuum on lowest possible suction, with layers of nylon net, fiberglass screening, or cheesecloth fastened firmly over the nozzle to keep the machine from sucking up the coverlet fabric. Do this to both faces of the coverlet — it may be the only cleaning the piece will need! If the coverlet is very strong and in excellent condition you can air it outdoors on a dry day — hang it carefully across two clean parallel clotheslines or bars and cover it with a large sheet to fend off sunlight, bird droppings, and other hazards. If the piece is still very dirty, you may need to wash it. Conservation labs do this by sandwiching the piece flat between layers of non-metal screening stretched in a frame. The frame can be lowered — still flat — into an immense shallow tank of tepid, pH-neutral water, jiggled gently up and down to work the water through the cloth, and lifted to drain. But chances are you don't have room in your basement or rec room for that kind of facility; the bathtub and your hands will have to suffice. First test the coverlet's colored yarns (by rubbing in an obscure spot with a wet white cloth or paper towel) to make sure they won't "bleed" color when wet. If they're okay, fold the coverlet to fit in the bathtub — but don't put it in yet. Run lukewarm water a few inches deep in the tub, dissolve a small amount of gentle soap (not detergent) in it, and lower the folded coverlet into it. With your hands flat, gently work the water through the piece to loosen the dirt. Do not squeeze, wring, twist, rub, or agitate the piece while it's wet — those activities and sudden changes of water temperature will make the wool shrink and felt and will break threads. Rinse the piece thoroughly by running lukewarm water through it until the water runs out clear. Let excess water drain out — you can gently press or squeeze to encourage the draining (but be prepared to get yourself damp when you lift the heavy wet coverlet). Wrap the piece in large towels to blot out excess water. Then spread it flat on a clean sheet in the shade, cover it with another sheet for protection, and let it air dry.

If you want to store your coverlet, the ideal way would be to roll it flat on a long cloth-covered tube, cover it with a loose cloth, and hang the whole roll horizontally by a rod through the tube. This method protects the coverlet from acid, dust, light, and strain. But if such storage is impractical, you can fold your fabric carefully and pad the insides of each fold with acid-free tissue paper (from a museum supply firm) or well-washed white sheeting. You should wrap it loosely in acid-free tissue or sheeting and shelve it in a dark closet where nothing else will be piled on top of it. Refolding it periodically is wise.

If you want to display your coverlet in your home, remember that worst-case scenario. Keep your coverlet away from the fireplace, furnace vents, windows, bright sunlight, the kitchen, frequently used furniture, dogs, cats, children, smokers, and any other hazards. If you're hanging it over a quilt rack or foot of a bed, be sure it is strong enough to hang, and pad inside and underneath the folds with white sheeting or acid-free tissue. If you plan to use the coverlet on a bed, choose a seldom-used guest bed in a room that is kept dim. Periodically clean the coverlet of settled dust, and remove it completely when the bed is to be used.

If your coverlet is strong enough to be hung for display, it must be well supported and should be hung flat. You can mount it on a strong fabric backing (like a well-washed white cotton sheet). Hand-stitch it to the backing with horizontal lines of running stitches, being careful to avoid splitting the coverlet's threads. Either stitch the backing to a cloth-wrapped wooden frame or make a heading in the backing and support the fabric with a strong rod through the heading. The backing should carry all of the coverlet's weight. Avoid hanging the coverlet where it will be handled or subjected to bright light.

If at all possible, don't cut up your coverlet. It may already be just a piece or a fragment or in ragged condition, but making it into pillows or framing it in wood will just destroy it faster. It may still be of interest "as is" to a coverlet researcher. So much original information about coverlets has been lost that most of what we know today has had to be deduced from the pieces themselves. After all, there will never be more 19th-century coverlets than exist today — only fewer!

Perhaps these suggestions for coverlet care seem restrictive, excessively conservative. But they are just that: conservative. They are measures you can take for conservation of your textile. It may be 125 or 150 years old and, like the rest of us, is not getting any younger. But if it's your coverlet, it's your choice. You need to balance how much you value the piece with what you want to do with it. And whatever you discover about your coverlet and decide to do with it, I hope you enjoy it!

A gathering of coverlets

This section presents the technical data (including drafts) and histories (if known) of almost all of the coverlets shown in this book.

A weaving pattern can be mapped on paper (by hand or with a computer program)—the result is called a *drawdown* or *fabric diagram*. The drawdowns of shaft-loomed patterns which illustrate this section were generated on an APPLE II+ computer. They were drawn using the WEFT-WRITER program, by Stewart Strickler of The Textile Tree. The summer & winter, doublefaced twill, and block double weave patterns are shown as block drawdowns; all others are thread-by-thread drawdowns. Drawdowns read from left to right, and from bottom to top—in other words, they show the lower lefthand corner of the border or pattern repeat.

The *pattern name*, if capitalized, is one which has been attributed to the design by a weaver or an author. A popular pattern which has several names is listed by the commonest title, with notation of some of the alternatives. In a few cases I have given an unnamed pattern a descriptive (uncapitalized) title, for convenience of reference.

The *pattern characteristics* item describes the way motifs are combined to form a particular pattern. Different specimens of a pattern may vary slightly—a rose might be simpler or fancier than usual, for example, or the blocks might all be enlarged or miniaturized. Sometimes the threading is usual but the treadling is not. When a pattern differs somewhat in one of these ways but is not distinctive enough to have its own name, I have called it a *variant*.

The *warp count* is the number of warp ends counted in one horizontal inch of the coverlet fabric.

Warp and *weft* yarns are listed by twist, ply, fiber, and color. Z and S indicate the direction of twist, comparable to the center angle (/ or \ ) of the letter. A designation of *two-ply* (Z *twist*, S *ply*) means "two strands, each of which is spun in Z direction, plied together in the S direction." For early hand-spinners and mill machines, Z-twist and S-ply were the norm.

Z-twist and S-twist refer to the direction in which a yarn and its component strands have been spun.

Size is the listing of the dimensions of the coverlet or fragment at the time it was documented.

Notes includes other documentation of the coverlet, pattern references, and history (if known). Unless otherwise designated, the coverlets shown here are privately owned.

For the convenience and pleasure of weavers, *drafts* are given here for the shaft-loomed coverlets. For the summer & winter, doublefaced twill, and block double weave patterns, the block (profile) draft form is used; the other techniques are represented with thread-by-thread drafts. In each case the drafts have been deduced from analysis of the coverlet itself or from close-up photos. Oddities (such as an imbalance of block sizes in an otherwise symmetrical design) and minor drafting errors have been retained, but threading errors and drafting idiosyncracies (such as disruption of the tabby order) have usually been eliminated. For the convenience of weavers I have included the number of warp ends or block units in a pattern repeat.

Each draft has three parts. At the top, the *threading* reads right to left. At the right of this is the *tie-up*, and below it the *treadling*, which reads from the top downwards. The threading and treadling are given for one repeat of the pattern, and, where relevant, for the entire border. If the treadling differs significantly from being "as drawn in" (with blocks treadled in the same order and proportion as they are threaded), the difference is noted in the text.

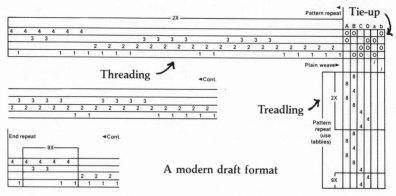

A modern draft format

I have used three different draft conventions. In a *thread-by-thread draft*, the numbers (as well as their position on the horizontal rows) in the threading represent the shafts on which the warps are to be threaded. Shaft 1 is closest to the weaver, and higher-numbered shafts are successive frames toward the back of the loom. The tie-up is "rising shed," with the **O**s in each column representing the shafts that are tied to be raised together by a treadle or set of levers. In the treadling the numbers represent the number of times in succession that the same treadle is to be used. If a background tabby weft is

97

required after each pattern weft shot, the treadling draft indicates *use tabbies*. Weft colors are also indicated in the draft where they are relevant.

In a *profile draft*, the letters represent groups of threads that act together as units, making blocks of pattern. Each weave structure has its own formula for threading, for tie-up, and for treadling, which a weaver can substitute in (or "plug into") the profile. These formulae are given with the notes on different block weaves in this section.

When the *blocks weave independently* in the pattern, I have used letters in the tie-up and treadling, with numbers in the treadling indicating the number of times a unit is repeated. When some of the *blocks weave combined* in the pattern I have used solid squares in the treadling to call attention to the fact that the tie-up is different.

Summer & winter formula

In the threading, each unit is a four-thread sequence on three shafts. The first end is on shaft 1, the third end on shaft 2, and the second and fourth ends are on one additional shaft. So block A is threaded 1, 3, 2, 3. Block B is threaded 1, 4, 2, 4. Block C is 1, 5, 2, 5. Block D is 1, 6, 2, 6.

In the tie-up, two treadles are tied for each block or block combination that will be used. One treadle raises shaft 1 and all the pattern shafts except those carrying the block; the other raises shaft 2 and the same pattern shafts. So the pair of treadles to weave block A are tied to raise 1-4-5-6 and 2-4-5-6. The pair to weave block B raise 1-3-5-6 and 2-3-5-6. The pair to weave blocks C and D together, for example, raise 1-3-4 and 2-3-4. The tabbies are 1-2 and 3-4-5-6-etc.

In the treadling, the pair of pattern treadles alternate, using tabbies. Four pattern and four tabby picks weave one unit square.

Block D		Block C		Block B		Block A	
6	6						
2		5	5				
				4	4		
						3	3
		2		2		2	
	1		1		1		1

Doublefaced twill formula

In the threading, each unit is a four-thread straight twill on four shafts. Block A is shafts 1 through 4. Block B is shafts 5-8. Block C is 9-12. Block D is 13-16.

In the tie-up, each set of four shafts is tied either as in I to weave pattern, or as in II to weave background.

Treadling is straight twill. One four-weft sequence squares each unit (no tabbies).

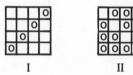

I   II

Block double weave formula

In the threading, each unit is a four-thread straight twill on four shafts, with the first and third ends light and the second and fourth ends dark. Block A is shafts 1 through 4. Block B is shafts 5-8. Block C is 9-12. Block D is 13-16.

In the tie-up, each set of four shafts is tied either as in I to weave the light layer on top and the dark layer beneath, or as in II to weave the dark layer on top and the light layer beneath.

The treadling alternates light and dark wefts in four-thread straight twill sequence. Four wefts (two light and two dark) square each unit, creating a two-by-two-thread square of plain weave on each layer.

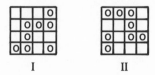

I   II

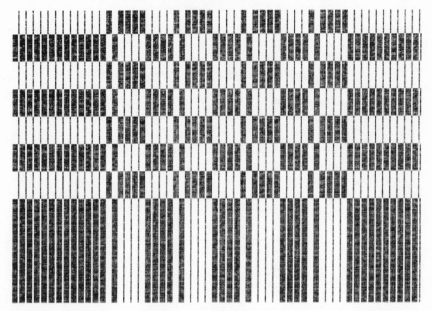

See also page 75.

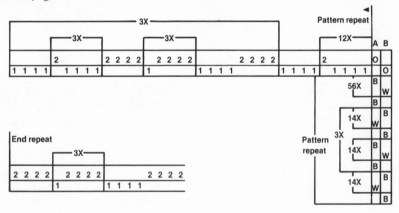

B = blue wool
W = white cotton

TREADLING: Not as drawn in
229 ends in pattern repeat.

Unnamed.

WARP COUNT: 35 e.p.i.

WARP: Very fine single-ply (Z-twist) cotton, natural.

WEFTS: *Light:* Same as warp. *Dark:* Single-ply (Z-twist) wool, blackish blue.

SIZE: Fragment 15½" (39 cm) square (2½ repeats square).

NOTES: This fragment was cut from a coverlet originally 66" (168 cm) wide, in two panels (one seam, not matched). The sides were selvedges; the ends were narrow hems. The fabric is not entirely weft-faced because the soft wool wefts spread to cover the warps but the harder fine cotton wefts do not. This piece is in the collection of the Denver Art Museum (1985.569).

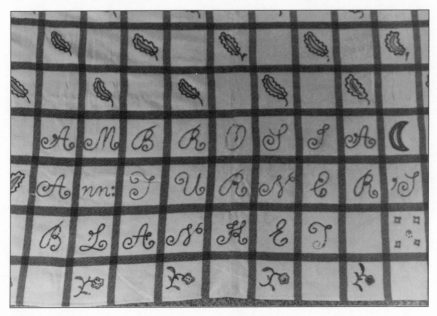

See also page 72.

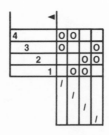

4 ends in a pattern repeat;
4¾" (12 cm) in a color repeat.

Embroidered checked blanket.

WARP COUNT: 28 e.p.i.

WARP & WEFT: Single-ply (Z-twist) wool, creamy natural and bright dark blue. Four-inch (10 cm) stripes and bands of natural and ¾" (2 cm) stripes and bands of blue. Embroidery in coral red, dark blue, and faded gold.

NOTES: The blanket is in two panels (one seam). The ends are narrow hems; the sides are selvedges. The blanket is in good condition. The natural-colored squares are embroidered. The side four rows read *ESTHER TURNER A.D. 1828*, and have a variety of horses, flowers, and birds. The bottom four rows read *AMBROSIA ANN TURNER'S BLANKET*, and have a simple flower. The central motif is a leaf, repeated in alternate natural-colored squares (the farther it is from the names, the simpler the leaf). The blanket was acquired from the owner's mother in Washington, D.C., about 1950, but its origin is unknown. As far as is known, Turner is not a family name. Family legend holds that Esther and Ambrosia were sisters and that Esther did her part of the embroidery but Ambrosia lost interest.

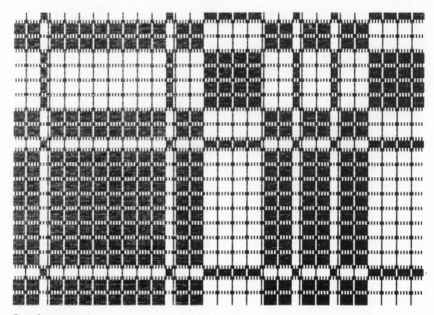

See also page 77.

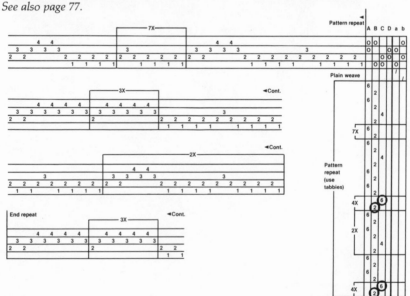

TIE-UP: Standard
284 ends in pattern repeat.

Only three blocks are threaded and treadled.
Circled numbers indicate red pattern weft;
all others are blue pattern weft.

Cloudless Beauty. A large table and four smaller tables, framing an area of nine stars. All figures are formed of equal-sized blocks, made predominantly from only two opposite blocks. As a result, there is very little "gray area" of incidentals.

WARP COUNT: 36 e.p.i.
WARP: Fine single-ply (Z-twist) cotton, natural.
WEFTS: *Tabby:* Same as warp. *Pattern:* Fine single-ply (Z-twist) wool, bright dark blue and tomato red.
SIZE: 60" wide by 79½" long (152 x 202 cm); 8 by 9¼ repeats.
NOTES: The Cloudless Beauty is one of the simple Patch patterns, where only two or three of the four possible overshot blocks are used.

This coverlet is in two panels (one seam, not matched, hand-sewn with ¼"/6 mm seam allowances). The ends are narrow hems; the sides are selvedges. The coverlet is worn but clean and whole. The coverlet is in the collection of the Denver Art Museum (1985.571), gift of Stewart and Carol Strickler.

FOUR-SHAFT OVERSHOT WEAVES

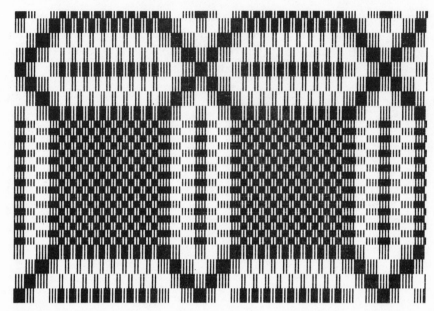

See also page 55.

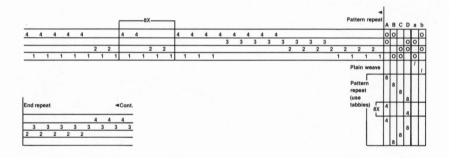

TIE-UP: Standard
TREADLING: As drawn in
124 ends in pattern repeat

Butternut. Large tables separated by a three-step cross (X).

WARP COUNT: 24 e.p.i.
WARP: Two-ply (Z-twist S-ply) cotton, natural.
WEFTS: *Tabby:* Single-ply (Z-twist) cotton, natural. *Pattern:* Two-ply (Z-twist S-ply) wool, uneven soft gold.
SIZE: Fragment 26″ wide by 27″ long.
NOTES: The ends are narrow hems; one side is selvedge and the other is cut. The coverlet is worn but whole.

See also page 54.

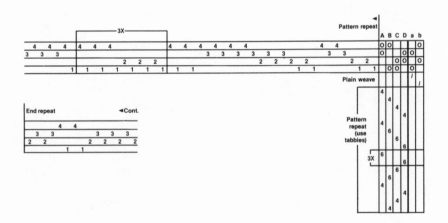

TIE-UP: Standard
TREADLING: As drawn in
86 ends in pattern repeat.

Orange Peel. Small tables separated by a seven-step cross (X), forming lozenge shapes between the tables.

WARP COUNT: 36 e.p.i.

WARP: Two-ply (Z-twist S-ply) cotton, natural.

WEFTS: *Tabby:* Single-ply (Z-twist) cotton, natural. *Pattern:* Single-ply (S-twist; hard twist) wool, dark blue.

SIZE: 56" wide by 92" long (142 x 234 cm); 16 by 20 repeats.

NOTES: This pattern is similar to Atwater draft #10, Swygert p. 39, and Burnham #241-42. The coverlet is in two panels (one seam, well matched vertically). The ends are overcast-stitched. The coverlet is firm and well woven, showing wear only at one end. It is in the Denver Art Museum (1965.309 A-726), gift of Mrs. F. H. Douglas.

See also page 53.

TIE-UP: Standard
TREADLING: As drawn in
348 ends in pattern repeat.

Bonaparte's March, also called Lily of the Valley or Rose in the Wilderness. A large garden motif, alternating with two dense tables that are separated by a small garden cross.

WARP COUNT: 20 e.p.i.

WARP: Two-ply (Z-twist S-ply) cotton, natural.

WEFTS: *Tabby:* Same as warp. *Pattern:* Two-ply (Z-twist S-ply) wool, bright dark blue.

SIZE: 73″ (185 cm) and two 6½″ (16.5 cm) fringes wide by 86½″ (220 cm) and one 6½″ (16.5 cm) fringe long.

NOTES: Bonaparte's March is another popular pattern, widely enough used that it had several different names.

   The coverlet is in two panels (one seam, well matched). The loom-woven quadruple fringe on the bottom and sides is unusually elaborate. It consists of four ⅝″ bands of pattern, hemstitched in groups of five ends on both edges, with ¾″ bands of five-by-five leno twists between bands and a 2″ warp fringe after the final pattern band. The coverlet is in good condition except for many snagged pattern wefts in the central area and for broken wool yarns no longer holding the leno twists in the open parts of the fringe. The coverlet's history is unknown, except that it came from a Maine family.

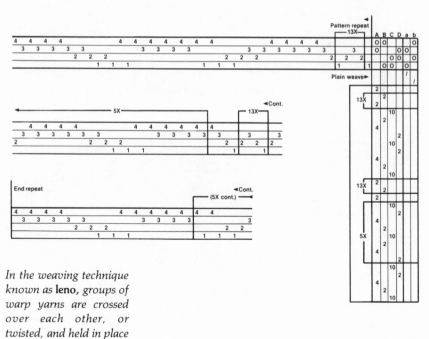

In the weaving technique known as **leno,** *groups of warp yarns are crossed over each other, or twisted, and held in place by a weft yarn.*

FOUR-SHAFT OVERSHOT WEAVES

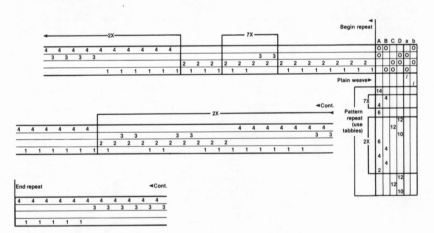

TIE-UP: Standard
TREADLING: As drawn in
218 ends in pattern repeat.

Fox Trail variant. A medium table and nine small two-step stars separated by small tables.

WARP COUNT: 40 e.p.i.
WARP: Fine single-ply (Z-twist) cotton, natural off-white.
WEFTS: *Tabby:* Same as warp. *Pattern:* Single-ply (Z-twist) wool, blackish blue.
SIZE: Fragments, one 13″ wide by 16″ long (33 x 40.5 cm), and one irregular.
NOTES: Irregular fragment is a piece of a panel 26″ (66 cm) wide with selvedge sides and very narrow twill-pattern border on one side. Two major threading errors were made when the loom was warped. The cloth is in extremely ragged and mended condition.

FOUR-SHAFT OVERSHOT WEAVES

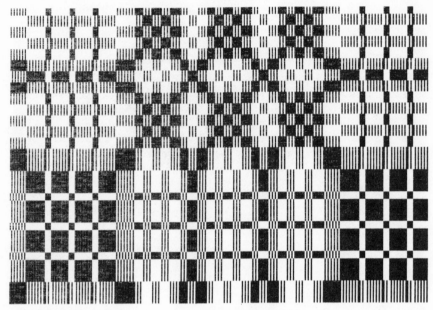

See also pages 35 and 51.

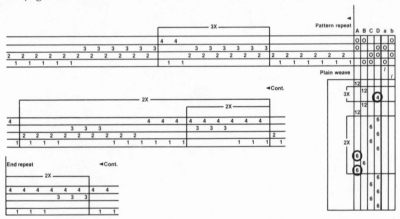

Circled numbers indicate red pattern wefts;
all others are blue pattern wefts.

TIE-UP: Standard
TREADLING: As drawn in
210 ends in pattern repeat.

114

Nine Stars & Table. A table on large and small opposite blocks, framed by incidentals, and nine stars separated by two-step crosses.

WARP COUNT: 39 e.p.i.

WARP: Fine single-ply (Z-twist) cotton, natural.

WEFTS: *Tabby:* Same as warp. *Pattern:* Single-ply (Z-twist) wool, very dark blue and pinkish red.

SIZE: 71" wide by 94" long (180 x 239 cm); 15 by 15½ repeats.

NOTES: This threading, if treadled rose-fashion, weaves Nine Snowballs or Dogtracks or Roses. The coverlet is in two panels (one seam, well matched but hand-sewn in a black running stitch with ⅜"/1 cm of each coverlet edge used in the seam). Approximately 1" (2.5 cm) has apparently been cut or torn off one selvedge. The top and bottom are badly torn narrow hems. The remaining fabric is in fairly good condition, except for some long slits where brittle threads broke when the coverlet was hung.

FOUR-SHAFT OVERSHOT WEAVES

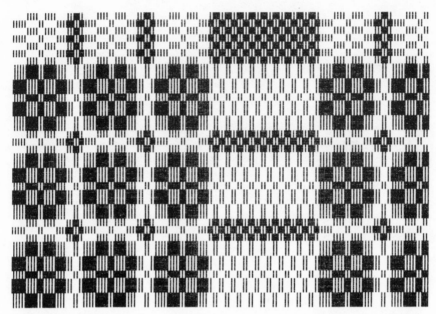

See also page 59.

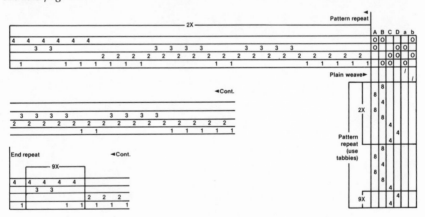

TIE-UP: Standard
TREADLING: Rose-fashion
206 ends in pattern repeat.

Nine Snowballs or Dogtracks. A table, and nine roses separated by two-step diamonds.

WARP COUNT: 30 e.p.i.
WARP: Two-ply (Z-twist S-ply) cotton, natural.
WEFTS: *Tabby:* Fine single-ply (Z-twist) cotton, natural. *Pattern:* Two-ply (Z-twist S-ply) wool, dark blue.
SIZE: 66" wide by 88½" long (168 x 225 cm); 10½ by 10½ repeats.
NOTES: This pattern is a rose-fashion treadling of a Nine Stars & Table draft. The coverlet is in two panels (one seam, well matched). The ends were originally hemmed, but all four edges are now bound with blue cotton percale binding. The pattern is the same as Hall p. 79, except for color.

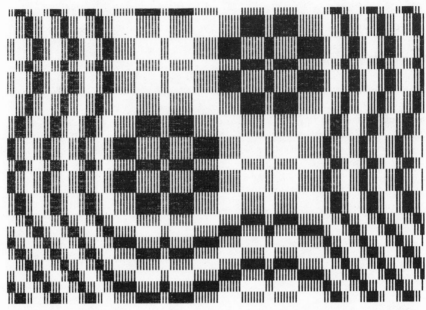

See also pages 30 and 34.

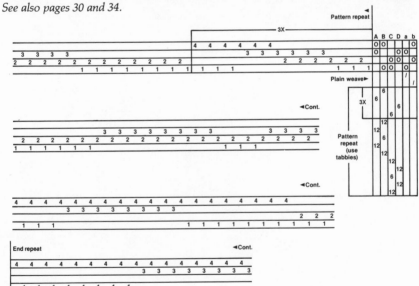

TIE-UP: Standard
TREADLING: Rose-fashion
212 ends in pattern repeat.

Cat Track & Snail Trail. Two alternating roses on opposing pairs of blocks, surrounded by three lines of diagonals.

WARP COUNT: 40 e.p.i.
WARP: Fine single-ply (Z-twist) cotton, yellowed natural.
WEFTS: *Tabby:* Same as warp. *Pattern:* Single-ply (Z-twist) wool, very dark blue.
SIZE: 89″ wide by 100″ long (226 x 254 cm); 13½ by 15½ repeats.
NOTES: This pattern, a popular one because it is so graphically named, is also found in variations called Rattlesnake or Wandering Vine.

This coverlet is in three panels (two seams, recently sewn). The ends are narrow hems; the sides are selvedges (one of which has shreds of heavy grayish-brown thread from originally being at the seam). There are two major and several minor threading errors in the weaving. The coverlet is in fairly good condition; it is whole and heavy, but has worn spots and a few holes.

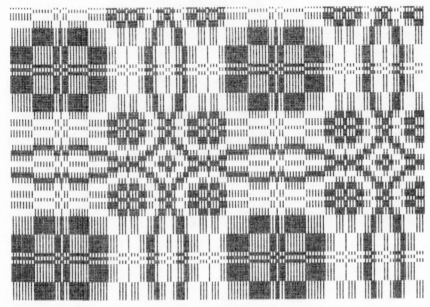

See also page 40, top center (lavender and black pattern).

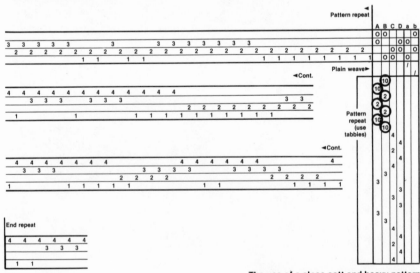

TIE-UP: Standard
TREADLING: Rose-fashion
146 ends in pattern repeat.

The use of a close sett and heavy pattern weft elongates the design more than is indicated in the drawdown.
Circled numbers indicate black pattern wefts; all others are red-violet.

Whig Rose. A large rose, framed by four small roses and surrounded by an indented ring.

WARP COUNT: 42 e.p.i.

WARP: Fine single-ply (Z-twist) cotton, very yellowed natural.

WEFTS: *Tabby:* Same as warp. *Pattern:* Single-ply (Z-twist) wool, in black and an uneven (mostly faded) light purple (see notes).

SIZE: 86″ wide by 95″ long (218 x 241 cm); 24 by 27 repeats.

NOTES: This coverlet represents an uncommon use of color in a common pattern. The design is similar to Hall pp. 136-37, Burnham #314, and Atwater drafts #69 and 91. It has also been one of the most popular overshot patterns for 20th-century reproduction coverlets.

The coverlet is in three panels (two seams, hand-stitched in a running stitch with narrow seam allowances, well matched except that one panel is reversed). One repeat of the pattern near the end of one panel is erroneously treadled star-fashion (as a Lover's Knot), instead of rose-fashion (as Whig Rose). The coverlet is in fair condition; it is worn, very faded in the purple areas, and yellowed by the black dye. The fading is slightly less noticeable toward one corner, and tiny hidden traces indicate that the purple was originally a bright red-violet or mauve, a possible indication of aniline dye and a post-1860 date.

See also page 29.

TIE-UP: Standard
TREADLING: As drawn in
232 ends in pattern repeat.

Whig Rose and Lover's Knot. A large rose, framed by four small roses and surrounded by an indented ring; a large star, framed by four small stars and surrounded by a convex ring. The two parts (star-fashion and rose-fashion of the same draft) alternate, connected by diamonds.

WARP COUNT: 18 e.p.i.

WARP: Two-ply (Z-twist S-ply) cotton, natural.

WEFTS: *Tabby:* Fine single-ply (Z-twist) cotton, natural. *Pattern:* Two-ply (Z-twist S-ply) cotton, natural.

SIZE: 74″ wide by 92″ long (188 x 234 cm).

NOTES: This coverlet is in two panels (one seam, well matched). The ends have been bound with fine white cotton fabric (on the straight grain), machine-stitched. The coverlet has been mended and patched in places.

The pattern is the alternating star and rose forms of Lover's Knot, forming the Whig Rose design between wheels. The use of all white cotton may indicate a Southern origin for this coverlet. It is #2-36A in the collection of the Boulder Historical Society, Boulder, Colorado, gift of Mrs. Frank Cattermole.

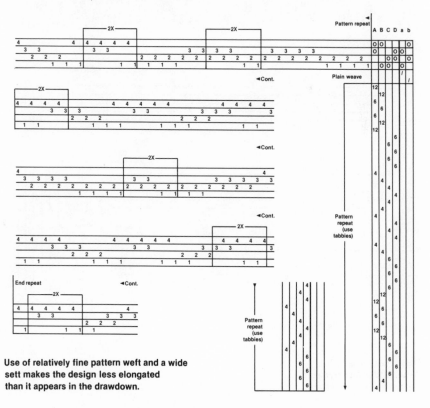

Use of relatively fine pattern weft and a wide sett makes the design less elongated than it appears in the drawdown.

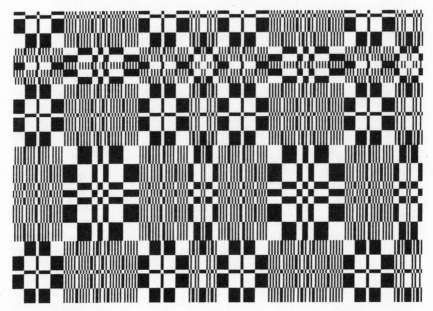

See also page 12.

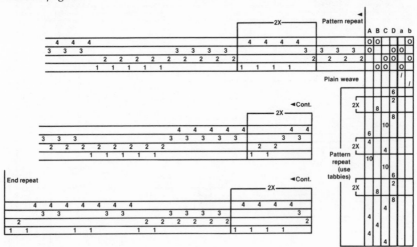

TIE-UP: Standard
TREADLING: Rose-fashion
140 ends in pattern repeat.

Whig Rose on opposite blocks: A large rose framed by four small roses and surrounded by an indented ring. All roses are drafted and treadled on opposite blocks, making a large background "gray area" of mixed incidentals.

WARP COUNT: 25 e.p.i.

WARP: Tightly spun two-ply (Z-twist S-ply) cotton, tannish natural.

WEFTS: *Tabby:* For 13" (33 cm) of one end of panel, same as warp. Remainder of panel is single-ply (Z-twist) short-fiber linen, golden tan. *Pattern:* Single-ply (Z-twist) wool, golden light brown.

SIZE: One panel (not measured) wider in linen tabby area than in cotton tabby area.

NOTES: Piece is one panel of a coverlet. It has been modified for use as a portière or curtain. Top has 2" (5 cm) hem for heading; bottom has a narrow hem; sides are selvedges. One side of the pattern has a narrow border. Pattern wefts are worn almost away in most places, although the cotton-tabby part is not as bad as the linen-tabby part. (This is possibly because of acidity of the brown dye, which has tinted the whole piece; also perhaps because the wool has been abraded by the harsher linen.) The panel is patched, but intact. The panel is a Connecticut family heirloom from Massachusetts, thought to have come originally from New Hampshire.

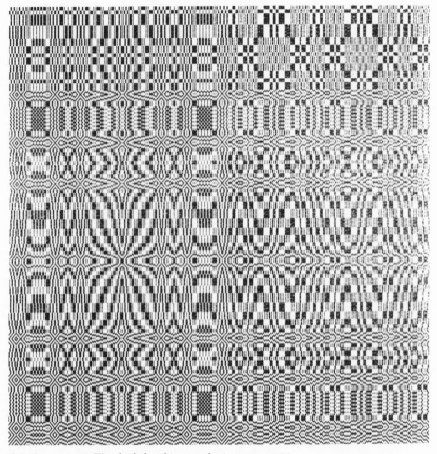

See also page 79. The draft for this coverlet is on page 128.

TIE-UP: Standard
TREADLING: As drawn in
116 ends in pattern repeat; 306 ends in border.

Lover's Knot on opposite blocks, with Double Bowknot/Chariot Wheel/Sunflower border. A large star, framed by four small stars and surrounded by a convex ring. All stars are drafted and treadled on opposite blocks, making a large background "gray area" of mixed incidentals. The border is a "hammerhead" diagonal, a small Sunflower motif, a cross, a small wheel, a cross, a Double Bowknot, a cross, a small wheel, a cross, a small Sunflower, and a cross — none of which is drafted on opposite blocks.

WARP COUNT: 20 e.p.i.
WARP: Unusual three-ply thread, possibly linen (two fine Z-twist and one thicker S-twist plies), shiny natural.
WEFTS: *Tabby:* Fine single-ply (Z-twist) cotton, natural. *Pattern:* Tightly spun two-ply (Z-twist S-ply) wool, dark blue.
SIZE: 81" wide by 88" long (206 x 223 cm); 9 repeats and two borders by 12 repeats and one border.
NOTES: The coverlet is in two panels (one seam, well matched). The top is a narrow hem; the bottom is cut off and raveled (and was apparently originally 1"/1.25 cm longer, with a plain-weave border and warp fringe). The sides are also narrow hems. The coverlet is in fairly good condition; it is whole and very heavy, but has torn areas.

Several things about this coverlet are unusual. One is the use of both cotton and linen (if the warp is, in fact, linen). Another is the pattern border, which is a combination of three other common motifs (a small Sunflower, a miniature Chariot Wheel, and a Double Bowknot, separated from each other by a stripe of point twill), none of which is on opposite blocks, as is the central design.

The coverlet is in the collection of the Denver Art Museum (1985.592), gift of Stewart and Carol Strickler.

Lover's Knot on opposite blocks, with Double Bowknot/Chariot Wheel/Sunflower border, described on pages 126-27.

Central Lover's Knot design is threaded and treadled on opposite blocks.

Pine Bloom, described on pages 130-131.

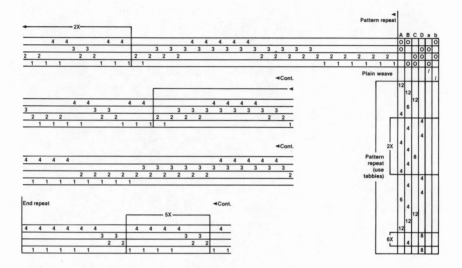

See also page 33. The draft for this coverlet is on page 129.

TIE-UP: Standard
TREADLING: As drawn in
246 ends in pattern repeat.

Pine Bloom. A large table of small and large opposite blocks framed by incidentals, and a "petal" area of alternately large and small crosses. Each petal has an asymmetrical, curved appearance, because the centers of the small crosses are one-directional threadings of opposite blocks.

WARP COUNT: 30 e.p.i.

WARP: Single-ply (Z-twist) cotton, natural.

WEFTS: *Tabby:* Same as warp. *Pattern:* Single-ply (Z-twist) wool, dark blue.

SIZE: 72″ wide by 84″ long (183 x 213 cm).

NOTES: This pattern is very popular; this version has a twill border on the bottom and sides. The coverlet is in two panels (one seam, well matched). It is worn and torn in places. It is in the collection of the Loveland Museum, Loveland, Colorado (74 A-2-12970), from the estate of Mrs. Clara Jennings. *Draft on page 129.*

WARP COUNT: 32 e.p.i.

WARP: Fine single-ply (Z-twist) cotton, yellowed natural.

WEFTS: *Tabby:* Same as warp. *Pattern:* Single-ply (Z-twist) wool, dark blue and faded dusky rose.

SIZE: Fragment 19½″ wide by 17″ long (50 x 43 cm); 2½ by 2 repeats.

NOTES: This fragment uses two colors of pattern weft to give the familiar Pine Bloom pattern a different look. The piece is in poor condition; it is worn and torn, with cut edges hand-hemmed on all four sides. It is thought to have been made by a former owner's maternal grandparents in about 1860. *Draft not given.*

WARP COUNT: 42 e.p.i.

WARP: Fine single-ply (Z-twist) cotton, natural.

WEFTS: *Tabby:* Same as warp. *Pattern:* Single-ply (Z-twist) wool, soft rose.

SIZE: Fragment 32″ wide by 53″ long (81 x 135 cm); 2½ by 4½ repeats.

NOTES: This piece is a variant of the popular Pine Bloom design, this time in a soft rose color that varies from moderate red to dark yellowish pink. The fragment is a shortened panel of a coverlet. The ends are narrow hems (one sewn with natural cotton and the other, probably not original, with pinkish cotton); the sides are selvedges. The fragment is intact but very worn, with the pattern wool worn away in many places. *Draft not given.*

WARP COUNT: 36 e.p.i.

WARP: Fine single-ply (Z-twist) cotton, natural.

WEFTS: *Tabby:* Same as warp. *Pattern:* Fine two-ply (Z-twist S-ply) wool, dark blue and strong reddish brown.

SIZE: Fragment 14″ wide by 13″ long (36 x 33 cm); 2 by 1½ repeats.

NOTES: This fragment is yet another variation of the Pine Bloom pattern, this time woven in dark blue and red. The fragment is cut on all four edges. There are threading and treadling errors in the weaving, and the fragment is in poor condition, both worn and mended. *Draft not given.*

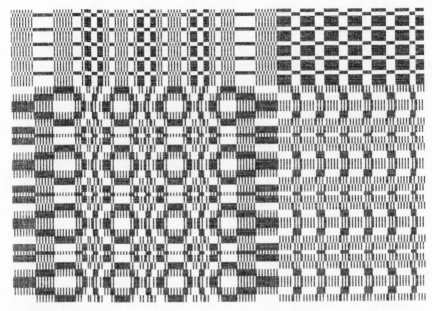

See also page 29.

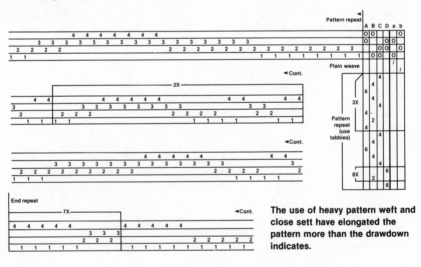

The use of heavy pattern weft and close sett have elongated the pattern more than the drawdown indicates.

TIE-UP: Standard
TREADLING: Rose-fashion, except for table motif
302 ends in pattern repeat.

Pine bloom treadled rose-fashion. The same as Pine Bloom, except that rose-fashion treadling of "petal" area forms small rings and teardrops.

WARP COUNT: 58 e.p.i.

WARP: Single-ply (Z-twist) cotton, tannish natural.

WEFTS: *Tabby:* Same as warp. *Pattern:* Single-ply (S-twist) wool, various dyelots of bright and blackish dark blue.

SIZE: 93" wide by 62" long (236 x 157 cm); 15 by 10 repeats.

NOTES: This coverlet is in three panels (two seams), and is wider than it is long. One panel is face up and two are face down; the seam between the two face-down panels is well matched but the other seam is not. The ends are narrow hems; the sides are selvedges. The coverlet is in excellent condition, except for one small hole.

This pattern is the popular Pine Bloom (also called Pine Burr, Sea Star, Isle of Patmos, and many other names), but in an unusual form. The "pine petal" part of the design is treadled rose-fashion, creating teardrop shapes. The coverlet was given to the owner's aunt in Warrenton, Virginia, in the 1920s and is possibly from Louden or Culpepper County, Virginia.

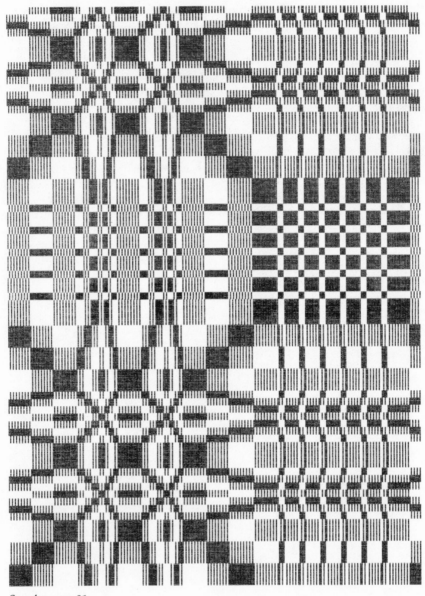

See also page 31.

TIE-UP: Standard
TREADLING: Nearly as drawn in
272 ends in pattern repeat.

Pine Bloom variant.

WARP COUNT: 34 e.p.i.

WARP: Fine single-ply (Z-twist) cotton, natural.

WEFTS: *Tabby:* Same as warp. *Pattern:* Single-ply (Z-twist) wool, possibly hand-spun, in tomato red, sage green (faded), and an unevenly faded purple.

SIZE: 62" wide by 71" long (157 x 180 cm); 8 by 9 repeats.

NOTES: This pattern is similar to most Pine Blooms (for example, Burnham #348-50 and Swygert p. 69). This design has only three solid blocks, instead of four, in the "pine petal" area, and the crosses between them are not on opposite blocks at their centers. The table is not treadled "square."

The coverlet is in two panels (one seam, matched, but the panels do not have half-repeats to balance the pattern across the seam). The ends are narrow, machine-stitched hems (apparently original), and the sides are selvedges. The coverlet is in fair condition; it is whole, but worn. The color (faded purple and green) and the hems (machine-stitched) may indicate a later date (1860s or after) for this coverlet.

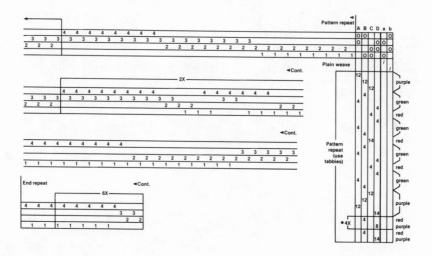

*Table is not squared in coverlet. To square, repeat 5X instead of 4X.

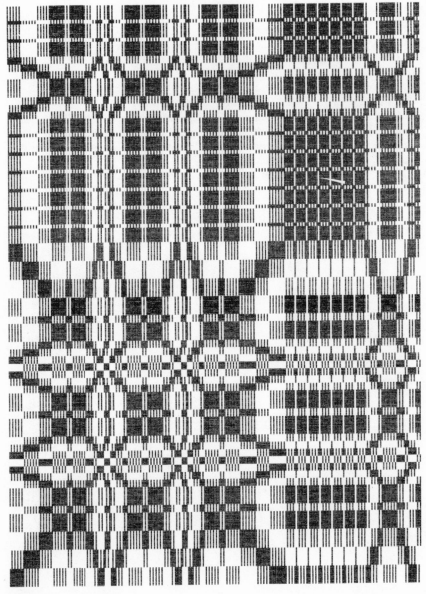

See also pages 53 and 59.

TIE-UP: Standard
TREADLING: As drawn in
330 ends in pattern repeat.

Gentleman's Fancy. The same as Pine Bloom, except that large crosses are elaborated into stars.

WARP COUNT: 29 e.p.i.
WARP: Uneven single-ply (Z-twist) cotton, natural.
WEFTS: *Tabby:* Same as warp. *Pattern:* Single-ply (S-twist) wool, tomato red and uneven dark olive green.
SIZE: 70½" (179 cm) and two fringes wide by 92" (234 cm) and two fringes long; 6 by 6½ repeats.
NOTES: Gentleman's Fancy is a Pine Bloom Pattern with stars instead of solid blocks in the "bloom" area. In this design, the table is also divided and is not on opposite blocks.

The coverlet is in two panels (one seam, well matched, but woven without half-repeats to balance the pattern across the seam). The ends have narrow hems; the sides are selvedges. All four edges have an applied tape-woven fringe of two-ply (S-twist Z-ply) wool (an unusual yarn) in about 10" (25.4 cm) bands of the same red and green as the coverlet. The fringe is woven on an eight-thread (⅓"/6 mm) warp of single-ply (S-twist) wool, red.

One end of the coverlet has an additional 4" (10 cm) length of fringe sewn diagonally across the corner. The coverlet was very well woven, and is in excellent condition since it has been washed carefully by the owner. It was part of a collection of overshot coverlets and hand-woven wool blankets "found" by a dog in a "rag heap" in a neighbor's shed. (The neighbor's reaction: "Oh, there's nothing worth anything in there—if you see something you want, take it, for goodness' sake!")

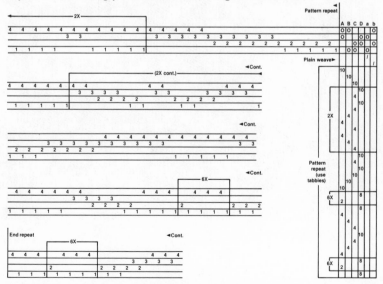

BREAKS IN THE TABBY ORDER HAVE BEEN CORRECTED IN THIS DRAFT.

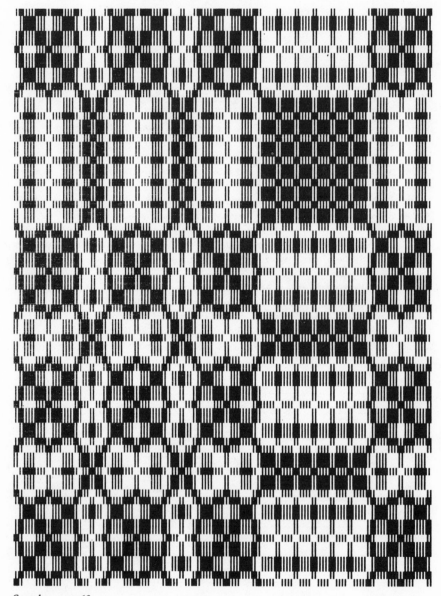

See also page 60.

TIE-UP: Standard
TREADLING: As drawn in
236 ends in pattern repeat.

Nine Chariot Wheels. Nine small wheels, separated by very small stars, alternated with a medium table.

WARP COUNT: 30 e.p.i.
WARP: Fine single-ply (Z-twist) cotton, natural.
WEFTS: *Tabby:* Same as warp. *Pattern:* Two-ply (Z-twist S-ply) wool, dark blue.
SIZE: 66" wide by 66" long (168 x 168 cm); 7½ by 7 repeats.
NOTES: The coverlet is in two panels (one seam, fairly well matched). It has been shortened and is very worn around the edges, which are torn on all four sides. It is patched in several places.

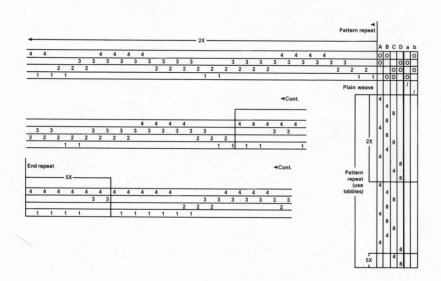

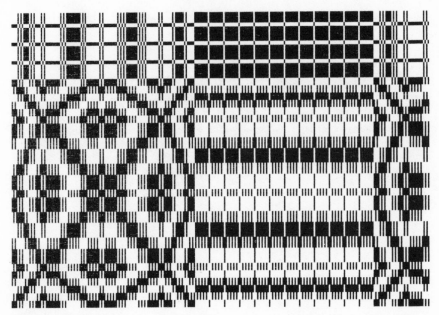

See also page 60.

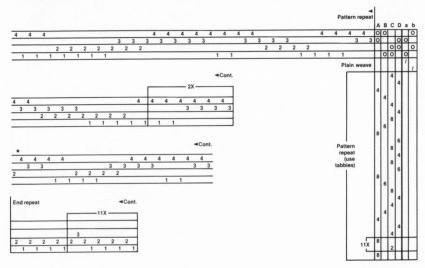

*Break in the tabby order.

TIE-UP: Standard
TREADLING: As drawn in
243 ends in pattern repeat

Chariot Wheel & Table. A large wheel with partial stars between the spokes, alternated with a large table on large and tiny opposite blocks.

WARP COUNT: 26 e.p.i.
WARP: Two-ply (Z-twist S-ply) cotton, natural.
WEFTS: *Tabby:* Single-ply (Z-twist) cotton, natural. *Pattern:* Fine two-ply (Z-twist S-ply) wool, dark blackish blue.
SIZE: Fragment 38″ wide by 41½″ long (96 x 105 cm); 3½ by 4 repeats.
NOTES: The fragment has the remains of the coverlet's center seam and ½″ (1.25 cm) of the adjoining panel on one side, and a thick ½″ (1.25 cm) hem on the other side. Its top and bottom edges are raveled warp fringes. The fragment is worn and torn. The piece was originally acquired in 1920 from a New Jersey woman who was about to discard it.

See also pages 57 (Governor's Garden) and 69 (Freemason's Felicity). The draft for this coverlet is on page 144.

TIE-UP: Standard
TREADLING: As drawn in
288 ends in pattern repeat.

Governor's Garden, also called Mountain Cucumber, St. Ann's Robe, and several other names. A garden motif, framed by four wheels, alternated with a table of equal-sized blocks.

WARP COUNT: 22 e.p.i.

WARP: Two-ply (Z-twist S-ply) cotton, natural.

WEFTS: *Tabby:* Single-ply (Z-twist) cotton, natural. *Pattern:* Two-ply (Z-twist S-ply) wool, dark and medium brown (thought to be dyed with walnut hulls) and dark gold (thought to be dyed with sumac).

SIZE: 70″ wide by 90″ long (178 x 229 cm).

NOTES: This pattern has many names and many variants. When the wheels at the corners are complete and symmetrical, it is sometimes called Freemason's Felicity (see listing under that name). The coverlet is in two panels (one seam, fairly well matched except that the brown dyelots differ on the panels). The ends are hemmed; the sides are selvedges. The coverlet is in good condition, except for frayed selvedges. The coverlet is in the collection of the Loveland Museum (74 A-5-121470), Loveland, Colorado. It came from the estate of Mrs. F. A. Lewis, once a Loveland resident.

According to the donor's history, "it was made in Ducksbury, Connecticut, by Mrs. Wm. Brown (Mrs. Lewis' great grandmother) in about 1800(?). The Browns, who were married just after the Revolutionary War, were friends of George Washington, and attended his inauguration ceremonies. After their Connecticut settlement was raided by Indians, the Browns went to New Hampshire to take up a grant by the Continental Congress. Mr. Brown was a Quaker, a descendent of Peter Brown of Plymouth." *Draft on page 144.*

Freemason's Felicity. A garden motif, framed by four complete wheels, alternated with a table of equal-sized blocks.

WARP COUNT: 28 e.p.i.

WARP: Fine two-ply (Z-twist S-ply) cotton, natural.

WEFTS: *Tabby:* Very fine single-ply (Z-twist) cotton, natural. *Pattern:* Two-ply (Z-twist S-ply) wool, dark blue.

SIZE: Fragment 10″ wide by 19″ long (25 x 48 cm); ½ by 1½ repeats.

NOTES: This pattern is one of a group of similar patterns known by a variety of names; see Governor's Garden. The true Governor's Garden pattern has wheels which are incomplete at the denser, ordinary table (see Atwater draft #23 and Swygert p. 66). Indian War has wheels which are incomplete at the "garden" table (see Atwater draft #22 and Swygert p. 65). Indian Review has no wheel rims, just Xs. Indian Plains has the wheels together, with no "garden" table, and the wheels are incomplete toward each other, like umbrellas (see Burnham #333). Freemason's Felicity is sometimes also called Chariot Wheel, or, if lacking a second table, Christian Ring.

All four edges of this fragment have been covered with crocheted shell edging made from off-white pearl cotton, doubled. The fragment is worn but intact; its wool is somewhat felted. The piece is in the collection of the Denver Art Museum (1985.572). *Draft not given.*

Governor's Garden

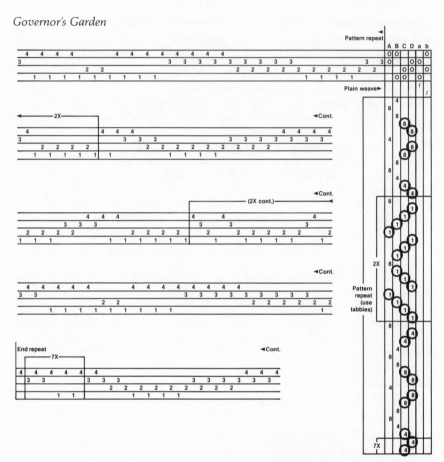

Circled numbers indicate brown pattern wefts; all others are gold.

See also page 70.

TIE-UP: Standard
TREADLING: As drawn in
528 ends in pattern repeat.

Tennessee Trouble. Diamond-shaped double wheels, alternated with a divided table.

WARP COUNT: 33 e.p.i.

WARP: Single-ply (Z-twist) cotton, natural.

WEFTS: *Tabby:* Same as warp. *Pattern:* Overtwisted single-ply (Z-twist) wool, uneven pinkish red and uneven light brown with blueish streaks in some areas.

SIZE: 74" wide by 90½" long (188 x 230 cm); 4½ by 5¼ repeats.

NOTES: This pattern is similar to Swygert p. 119, Hall pp. 142-43, and Atwater draft #54. The coverlet is in two panels (one seam, well matched although sewn with heavy black thread). The ends are narrow hems; the sides are selvedges. The coverlet is whole but very worn, with frayed edges. The piece is a family heirloom, taken to Colorado from Tennessee in 1904.

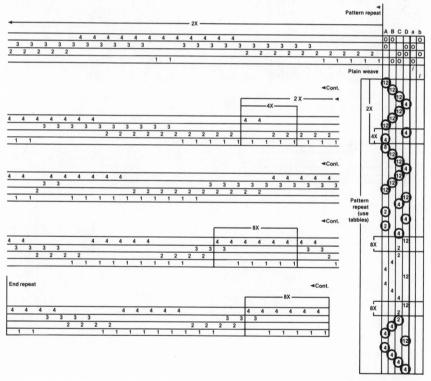

Circled numbers indicate brown pattern wefts; all others are red.

147

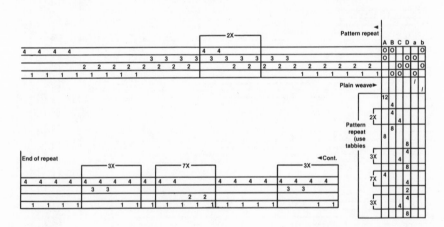

TIE-UP: Standard
TREADLING: As drawn in
178 ends in pattern repeat.

148

Catalpa Flower or Work Complete. The Catalpa Flower is a Sunflower-type pattern. The blossom (a table flanked by four stars which incorporate one of the table's blocks, framed by the table's other block) alternates with a star.

WARP COUNT: 28 e.p.i.
WARP: Fine single-ply (Z-twist) cotton (irregularly spun), yellowed natural off-white.
WEFTS: *Tabby:* Same as warp. *Pattern:* Heavy single-ply wool (Z-twist), dark blue and brick red.
SIZE: Fragment 14½" wide by 15" long (37 x 38 cm).
NOTES: The fragment has narrow hems on top, bottom, and one edge. The pattern is well woven, with color bands accentuating parts of the pattern.

FOUR-SHAFT OVERSHOT WEAVES

See also page 57.

TIE-UP: Standard
TREADLING: As drawn in
314 ends in pattern repeat.

Sunrise. A small sunrise motif and a dense table, divided by a garden cross.

WARP COUNT: 24 e.p.i.

WARP: Two-ply (Z-twist S-ply) cotton, natural.

WEFTS: *Tabby:* Fine single-ply (Z-twist?) cotton. *Pattern:* Heavy, very even two-ply (Z-twist S-ply) wool, reddish brown and dark mustard.

SIZE: 73" wide by 96½" long (185 x 245 cm); 5½ by 6 repeats.

NOTES: This coverlet is the one shown in DeGraw #76-77 and is like the patterns in Davison and Mayer-Thurman pp. 24-25, Hall pp. 374-75, Swygert p. 31, and Burnham #249. The coverlet is in two panels (one seam, well matched and sewn). Selvedges have been later buttonhole-stitched with a shinier (mercerized) white cotton two- or three-ply thread. There are narrow hems on both ends. The coverlet is in excellent condition, except for an occasional snagged pattern weft. The coverlet is in the collection of the Denver Art Museum (1958.63).

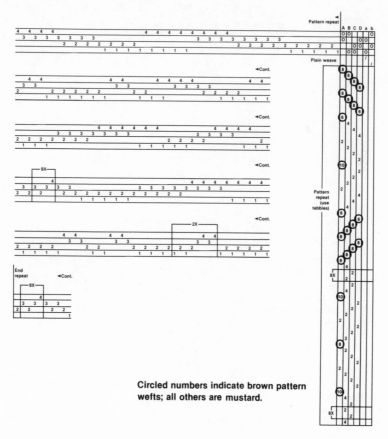

Circled numbers indicate brown pattern wefts; all others are mustard.

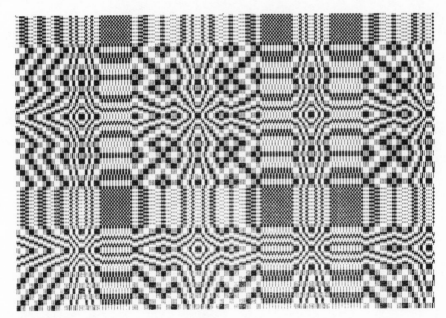

See also page 56.

TIE-UP: Standard
TREADLING: As drawn in
306 ends in pattern repeat; 240 ends in border.

Sunrise variant. A small sunrise motif with hammerheads, and a dense table divided by a garden cross.

WARP COUNT: 27 e.p.i.

WARP: Two-ply (Z-twist S-ply) cotton, natural.

WEFTS: *Tabby:* Uneven single-ply (Z-twist) cotton, natural. *Pattern:* Heavy two-ply (Z-twist S-ply) wool, at least two dyelots of very dark blue.

SIZE: 78½" wide by 83½" long (199 x 212 cm); 5 repeats and two borders by 5½ repeats and one border.

NOTES: This coverlet is in two panels (one seam, well matched). The panels have been assembled with the side borders along the center seam instead of at the edges. The sides are selvedges; the top and bottom have been cut and bound with narrow binding of very fine tan fabric (possibly linen) which is very worn. Except for the worn area and a small tear near the side of one panel, the coverlet is in good condition. It was said to have been woven by Mary Pugh Chenoweth (born January 29, 1762, married February 1, 1779, died February 1, 1849). Mary's husband was a Revolutionary War veteran. "Of the 'spreads' handed down in the family since, this one is thought to be the oldest because it shows the most wear." In the collection of the Denver Art Museum (1985.574), gift of Stewart and Carol Strickler.

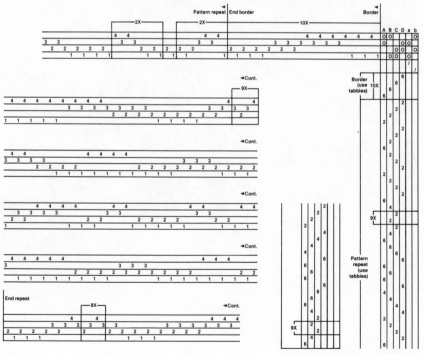

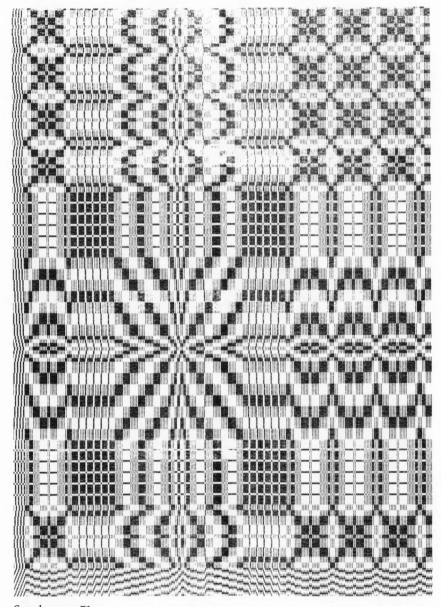

See also page 71.

TIE-UP: Standard
TREADLING: As drawn in
60 ends in pattern repeat; 365 ends in border.

154

Lee's Surrender. Repeated stars, separated by a tiny two-step cross. Border of twill, a star, a table on opposite blocks, a sunrise, and a table.

WARP COUNT: 34 e.p.i.

WARP: Two-ply (Z-twist S-ply) cotton, natural.

WEFTS: *Tabby:* Same as warp. *Pattern:* Single-ply (Z-twist) wool, possibly handspun, uneven dark and medium blue.

SIZE: 68″ wide by 99″ long (173 x 251 cm); 25 stars and two borders by 34 stars and two borders.

NOTES: This pattern is similar to Hall pp. 28-29, Atwater draft #107 and p. 68, and Swygert p. 121. The coverlet is in two panels (one seam, well matched). The ends are narrow plain-weave hems (blue wool weft); the sides are selvedges. There are threading and treadling errors in the weaving. The coverlet is in fairly good condition, whole but with areas of worn pattern wefts. It is thought to have been woven by the owner's mother-in-law, Frances Church Van Pelt, in Berea, Kentucky, in the 1920s, but the yarns are the typical old ones and the coverlet may in fact be an older piece that she acquired in that area.

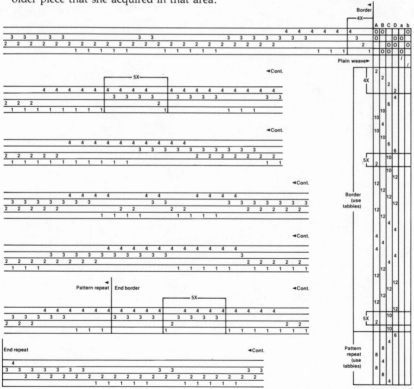

155

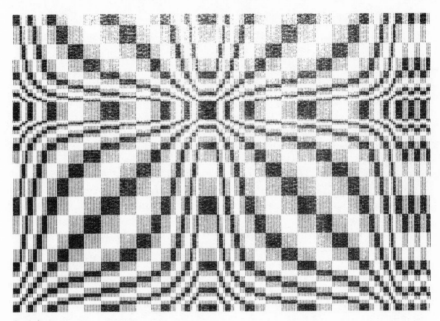

See also page 58.

TIE-UP: Standard
TREADLING: As drawn in
606 ends in pattern repeat.

Double Bowknot. A large bowknot motif.

WARP COUNT: 42 e.p.i.

WARP: Fine single-ply (Z-twist) cotton, natural.

WEFTS: *Tabby:* Same as warp. *Pattern:* Single-ply (Z-twist) wool, bright dark blue.

SIZE: 66″ wide by 100″ long (168 x 254 cm); 4½ by 5½ repeats.

NOTES: For the pattern, see Swygert p. 34. This example uses very large blocks (some with skips as long as twenty-six threads) and fine threads. The coverlet is in two panels (one seam, well matched). The ends are the remains of narrow hems; the sides are selvedges. The coverlet is in fairly good condition, although worn and torn in spots. The piece is a family heirloom, from Tennessee in 1960, from a branch of the family that has been in Tennessee since 1812.

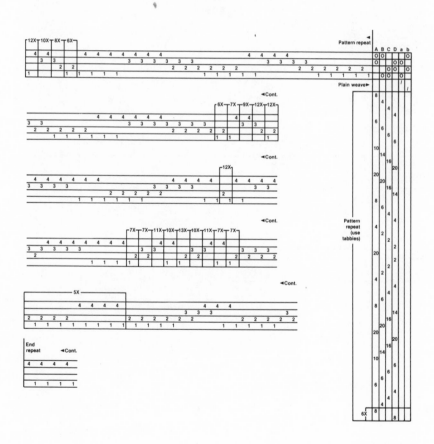

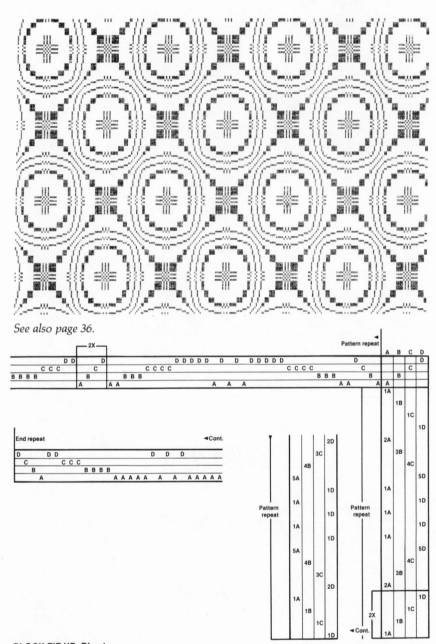

See also page 36.

BLOCK TIE-UP: Direct
BLOCK TREADLING: As drawn in
82 units in pattern repeat.

Wheel of Fortune, also called Cup & Saucer. Alternate star and rose forms of the same motif, connected by diagonals that form rings around the roses.

WARP COUNT: 26 e.p.i.

WARP: Fine two-ply (Z-twist S-ply) cotton, natural.

WEFTS: *Tabby:* Fine single-ply (Z-twist) cotton, natural. *Pattern:* Tightly plied two-ply (Z-twist S-ply) wool, bright dark blue.

SIZE: Two panels, each 36″ wide by 100″ long (91 x 254 cm); each 3 by 7 repeats.

NOTES: This pattern, one of several popular ones in which the star and rose motifs alternate, is also found in four-shaft overshot.

The panels are two halves of a coverlet. The ends are narrow hems; the sides are selvedges. There are some treadling and shuttle-skip errors. The coverlet is in good condition, with some small worn spots. The pieces were discovered at the same estate sale as the red, five-block Snowball & Four Roses summer & winter coverlet shown on pages 162-63 — a real treasure-find!

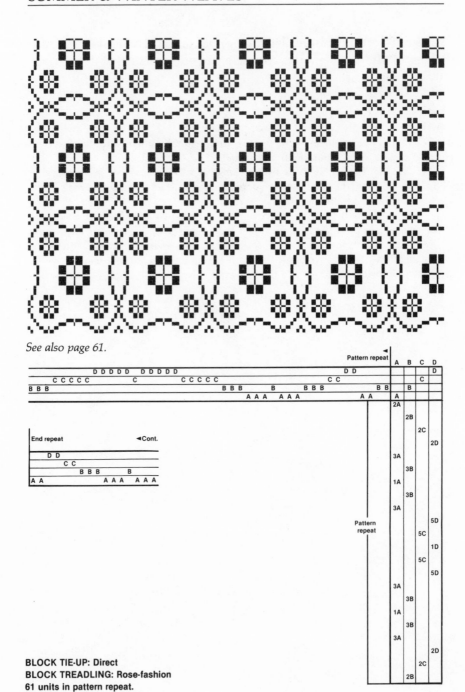

See also page 61.

Pattern repeat

		A	B	C	D
D D D D D D D D D D	D D				D
C C C C C C C C C C C	C C			C	
B B B	B B B B B B B	B B	B		
A A A A A A	A A	A			

End repeat ◄Cont.

D D	
C C	
B B B B	
A A A A A A A A	

BLOCK TIE-UP: Direct
BLOCK TREADLING: Rose-fashion
61 units in pattern repeat.

Whig Rose. A large rose, flanked by four small roses and surrounded by an indented ring.

WARP COUNT: 40 e.p.i.

WARP: Two-ply (Z-twist S-ply) cotton, natural.

WEFTS: *Tabby:* Single-ply (Z-twist) cotton, natural. *Pattern:* Two-ply (Z-twist S-ply) wool, dark blue.

SIZE: 70" wide by 85" long (178 x 216 cm); 6 by 5⅓ repeats.

NOTES: The Whig Rose pattern, familiar in four-shaft overshot, has here been used as a block design in summer & winter weave. Similar coverlets are Burnham #263 and Swygert p. 199. The coverlet is in two panels (one seam, only fairly well matched). The ends are hems and the sides are selvedges. It is in good condition.

Some authors have said that summer & winter weave was used primarily by Pennsylvania Germans, but Gehret says that's untrue; so even this coverlet's general history is unknown. It is in the collection of the Denver Art Museum (1984.779), gift of Stewart and Carol Strickler.

See also pages 8, 36, 37, and 81.

BLOCK TIE-UP: Combined
BLOCK TREADLING: As drawn in
43 units in pattern repeat; 55 units in border.

Single Snowball & Four Roses, with Pine Tree border. A solid fancy snowball, flanked by four roses and surrounded by an indented ring. The border is made of triple-trunked pine trees, which are extensions of the snowball.

WARP COUNT: 22 e.p.i.

WARP: Two-ply (Z-twist S-ply) cotton, natural.

WEFTS: *Tabby:* Single-ply (Z-twist) cotton, natural. *Pattern:* Two-ply (Z-twist S-ply) wool, uneven dusky rose-red.

SIZE: 39″ wide by 95″ long (99 x 241 cm); 4 repeats and one border by 11 repeats and one border.

NOTES: This pattern is like a Whig Rose, but with a Snowball center. It is similar to Swygert p. 211, Atwater draft #225, and other double weave designs. The piece is one panel (half a coverlet). The ends are narrow plain-weave hems; the sides are selvedges. It is in good condition, except for wear on the hems and at a few other small spots.

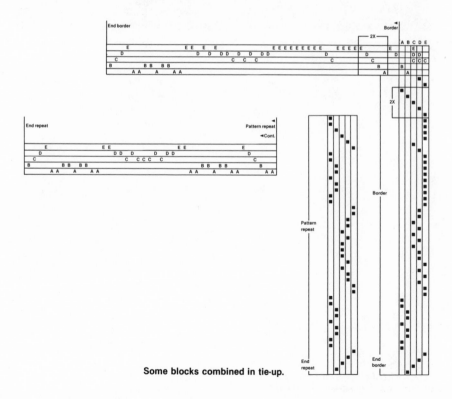

Some blocks combined in tie-up.

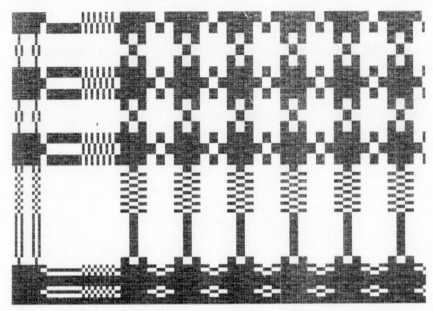

See also pages 27, 40, and 81 (on page 40 this is the navy-and-white coverlet).

BLOCK TIE-UP: Direct
BLOCK TREADLING: Nearly rose-fashion
18 units in pattern repeat; 37 units in border.

Nine-Patch, with Pine Tree border. Solid squares of color, alternated with nine-part squares. The border pine trees are extensions of the dark stripes and bands.

WARP COUNT: 24 e.p.i.

WARPS & WEFTS: *Light:* Four-ply (Z-twist S-ply) cotton, yellowed natural. *Dark:* Tightly plied two-ply (Z-twist S-ply) wool, dark blackish blue.

SIZE: 36" (91 cm) and one 5" (13 cm) fringe wide by 79" (200 cm) and one 5" (13 cm) fringe long; 8½ repeats and one border by 22½ repeats and one border.

NOTES: The piece is one panel (half a coverlet). The top is a narrow hem; the seam side is selvedge; the border side is unanchored weft-loop fringe (all wefts); the bottom is unanchored warp fringe (all warps). The panel is in excellent condition, except for a 7" (18 cm) streak of holes along an apparent middle crosswise fold. The dealer from whom it was acquired had purchased it in Ohio.

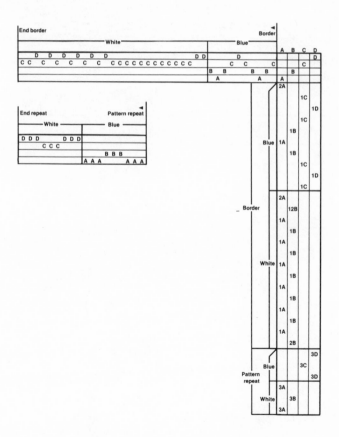

See also page 55.

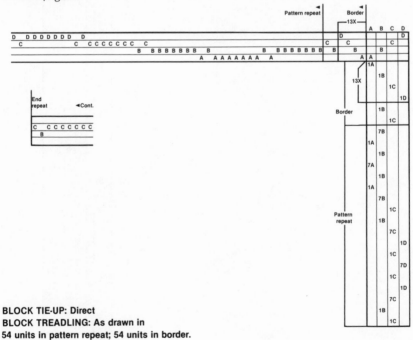

BLOCK TIE-UP: Direct
BLOCK TREADLING: As drawn in
54 units in pattern repeat; 54 units in border.

Diamond blocks. Line-edged squares in diagonal rows that form diamonds of background. The border is made of parallel narrow diagonal lines.

WARP COUNT: 34 e.p.i. (17 in each layer).

WARPS & WEFTS: *Light layer:* Two-ply (Z-twist S-ply) cotton, natural. *Dark layer:* Two-ply (Z-twist S-ply) wool, dark blue.

SIZE: 65" wide by 77" long (165 x 196 cm); 8½ repeats and two borders by 12 repeats and one border.

NOTES: This same coverlet is DeGraw #90-91. The pattern is an elaboration of Swygert p. 170 and Atwater draft #178, with borders on the sides and one end. The coverlet is in two panels (one seam, well matched). The ends are narrow hems; the sides are selvedges. The coverlet is in excellent condition, except for a little wear near the ends. It is in the collection of the Denver Art Museum (1932.14 A-165). It was the gift of Mrs. Effie Parkhill.

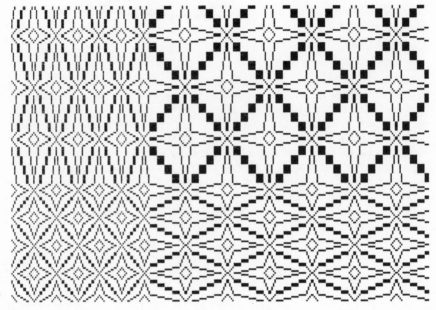

See also page 62.

BLOCK TIE-UP: Direct.
BLOCK TREADLING: Inverted
56 units in pattern repeat; 90 units in border.

Star of Bethlehem with border. The Star of Bethlehem motif is formed with twelve-step diagonals that are small, large, and small, intersecting to make diamonds, each of which contains a four-pointed star. The border is a smaller Star of Bethlehem.

WARP COUNT: 36 e.p.i.

WARPS & WEFTS: *Light layer:* Two-ply (Z-twist S-ply) cotton, natural. *Dark layer:* Two-ply (Z-twist S-ply) wool, dark blue.

SIZE: Fragment 12″ wide by 17″ long (30 x 43 cm); 1 repeat and one border by 2 repeats and one-half border.

NOTES: The Star of Bethlehem pattern, familiar in four-shaft overshot, has here been used as a block pattern for double weave. The borders intersect to form smaller stars in the corner. The treadling has been inverted (rose-fashion, switching block A with block D and block C with block B). The fragment has cut edges on both ends and one side; the border side is selvedge. It is in good condition. The fragment is in the study collection of the San Diego Creative Weavers Guild, San Diego, California.

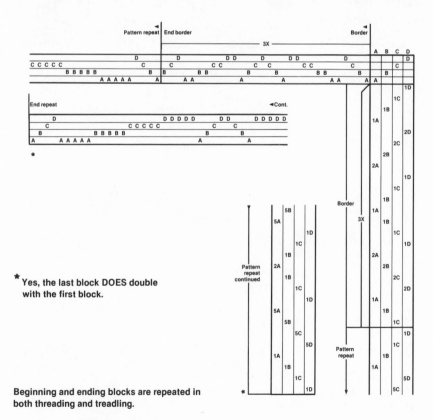

* **Yes, the last block DOES double with the first block.**

Beginning and ending blocks are repeated in both threading and treadling.

BLOCK DOUBLE WEAVES

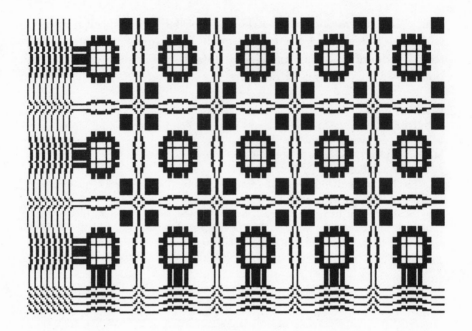

BLOCK TIE-UP: Combined
BLOCK TREADLING: As drawn in
52 units in pattern repeat; 37 units in border

A rose or snowball. A large, open snowball flanked by four squares and surrounded by an indented ring. The border is a triple-trunked pine tree, formed by extending one side of the snowball.

WARP COUNT: 32 e.p.i. (16 wool layer and 16 cotton layer).
WARPS & WEFTS: *Cotton:* Two-ply (Z-twist S-ply), natural off-white. *Wool:* Two-ply (Z-twist S-ply; very fine plies), uneven dark blue to blackish blue.
SIZE: Two fragments approximately 13" wide by 15" long (33 x 38 cm).
NOTES: The cotton layers of the fragments are so ragged that the pattern could only be deduced from the treadling of the border where it was more intact. The wool (blue) part of the cloth is still firm and indicates an originally well-woven coverlet.

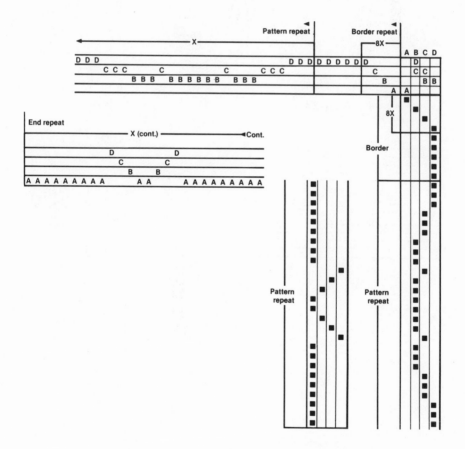

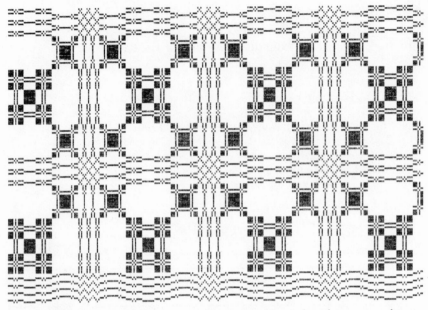

See also pages 40, 50, and 83 (on page 40 this is the white, red, and green coverlet at lower center).

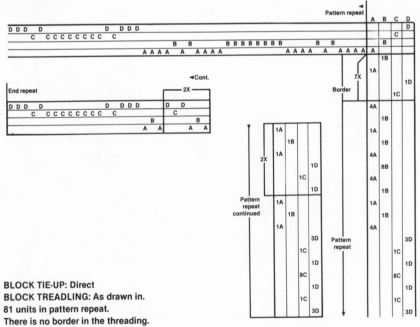

BLOCK TIE-UP: Direct
BLOCK TREADLING: As drawn in.
81 units in pattern repeat.
There is no border in the threading.

Unnamed tables and diamonds. A large center table (formed of double stars with a square in the center), flanked by four stars and separated by small diamonds.

WARP COUNT: 38 e.p.i. (19 in each layer).

WARPS & WEFTS: *Light layer:* Two-ply (Z-twist S-ply) cotton, creamy natural. *Dark layer:* Two-ply (Z-twist S-ply) wool, unevenly dyed tomato red and grayish blue-green.

SIZE: 84" (213 cm) wide by 86½" (220 cm) and one 3" (8 cm) fringe long; 9½ repeats by 9½ repeats and one border.

NOTES: This pattern uses a direct tie-up (one block at a time) and as-drawn-in treadling. If the tie-up were, instead, rose-fashion with some blocks combined, the design would be an unusual Snowball with Four Roses (see below). The coverlet is in two panels (one seam, very well matched). The top is cut and bound with fine olive-tan ¾"/2 cm point-twill tape (possibly linen). The sides are selvedges; the bottom has knotted warp fringe, with both warp layers tied together into fourteen-thread overhand knots and the cotton ends trimmed (or worn) off. The piece is whole, but badly worn. The cotton layer has been worn away at the top, along the selvedges, along the seam, and in large areas along the center of each panel. A 3" by 4" (8 x 10 cm) piece is torn out of the lower edge.

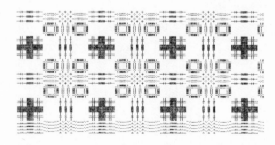

The A and B blocks are threaded and treadled with red in the wool layer; blocks C and D are threaded and treadled with green in the wool layer. The cotton layer is all white in all blocks.

BLOCK DOUBLE WEAVES

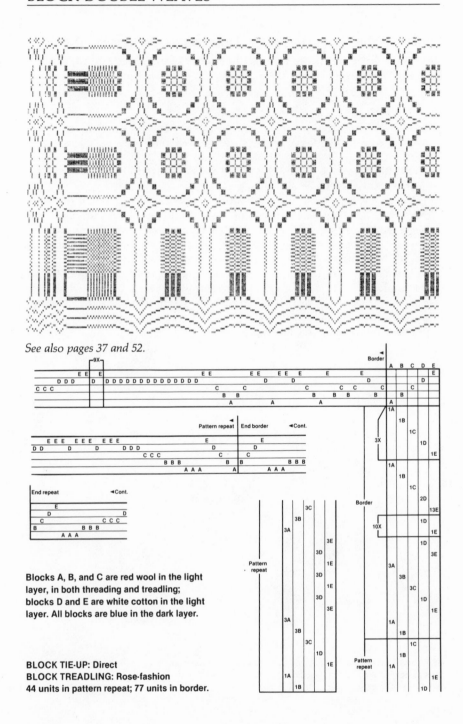

See also pages 37 and 52.

Blocks A, B, and C are red wool in the light
layer, in both threading and treadling;
blocks D and E are white cotton in the light
layer. All blocks are blue in the dark layer.

BLOCK TIE-UP: Direct
BLOCK TREADLING: Rose-fashion
44 units in pattern repeat; 77 units in border.

Snowball & Ring, with Pine Tree border. An open snowball, surrounded by a convex ring and separated by a four-pointed star. The border is a triple-trunked pine tree (an extension of the snowball), framed by an arch (an extension of the ring).

WARP COUNT: 40 e.p.i. (20 in each layer).

WARPS & WEFTS: *Light layer:* Two-ply (Z-twist S-ply) cotton, natural, and two-ply (Z-twist S-ply) wool, very unevenly faded brick red. *Dark layer:* Two-ply (Z-twist S-ply) wool, dark blue.

SIZE: 35" wide by 95" long (89 x 241 cm); 5½ repeats and one border by 18½ repeats and one border.

NOTES: This piece is one panel (half a coverlet). According to a former owner, the other half was destroyed when it was washed in a washing machine. The pattern includes a half-repeat at the inner edge and would probably have been well matched. The top is a narrow hem; the bottom is warp fringe (both warps); the sides are selvedges (separate layers). There are minor flaws in threading and treadling. At one time, wire rings were sewn at 3" (7.6 cm) intervals across the panel 18" (46 cm) from the top end, apparently so the panel could be hung as a curtain. The rings were corroding and staining the fabric green, and have been removed. The panel is in good condition, although worn and torn in spots.

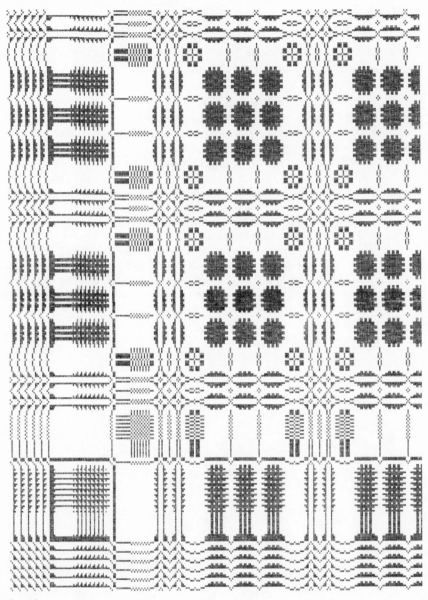

See also page 64.

BLOCK TIE-UP: Combined.
BLOCK TREADLING: As drawn in.
101 units in pattern repeat; 97 units in border.

Nine Snowballs & Four Roses, with double Pine Tree borders. Nine solid snowballs, separated by a tiny two-step diamond and flanked by four roses, the whole surrounded by indented rings that form four-pointed stars where they meet. The outer border is three triple-trunked pine trees (extensions of the snowballs), with flanking pairs of hollow trees (extensions of the four-pointed stars). The inner border is two baseless, double-trunked pine trees (extensions of the roses), with very slender trees in between (extensions of the tiny diamonds).

WARP COUNT: 36 e.p.i. (18 in each layer).

WARPS & WEFTS: *Light layer:* Two-ply (Z-twist S-ply) cotton, natural. *Dark layer:* Two-ply (Z-twist S-ply) wool, dark blue.

SIZE: 64" wide by 71" long (163 x 180 cm) plus fringe.

NOTES: The main pattern is similar to a Single Snowball in Burnham (#410), and to a Nine Snowballs (with less elaborate division) in Davison & Mayer-Thurman (#46) and in Swygert (p. 178), as well as to several drafts in Atwater (pp. 230-32). The coverlet is in two panels (one seam, well matched but the sewing is obtrusive). The bottom has warp fringe (both warps) and the top has a narrow hem. The coverlet is in excellent condition, except that improper washing has made the blue dye run slightly into the surrounding white cotton and has caused the wool layer to shrink and become felted, puckering the cotton layer.

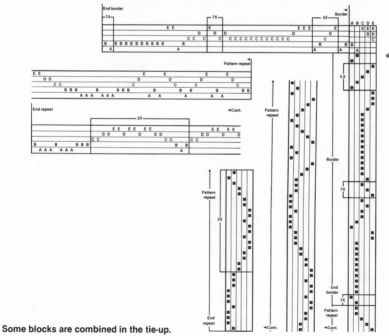

Some blocks are combined in the tie-up.

177

BLOCK DOUBLE WEAVES

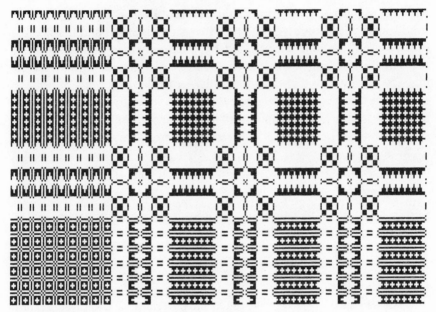

See also page 56.

BLOCK TIE-UP: Combined
BLOCK TREADLING: As drawn in
72 units in pattern repeat; 69 units in border.

Wheels and forty-nine slates. Seven-by-seven table of slates, alternated with four small wheels that are separated by quarter-rings that form a diamond "knot" where they meet. The border is made of outlined negative squares which enclose two-step solid diamonds.

WARP COUNT: 34 e.p.i. (17 in each layer).
WARPS & WEFTS: *Light layer:* Two-ply (Z-twist S-ply) cotton, yellowed natural. *Dark layer:* Two-ply (Z-twist S-ply) wool, possibly hand-spun, dark blue.
SIZE: 74" wide by 90" long (188 x 229 cm) plus fringe.
NOTES: This pattern is very intricate, with wheels, slates, and a wide border on the sides and bottom. The coverlet is in two panels (one seam, well matched). The top is a narrow hem; the sides are selvedges; the bottom has a 3" (8 cm) warp fringe which includes both layers, although the cotton has worn away.

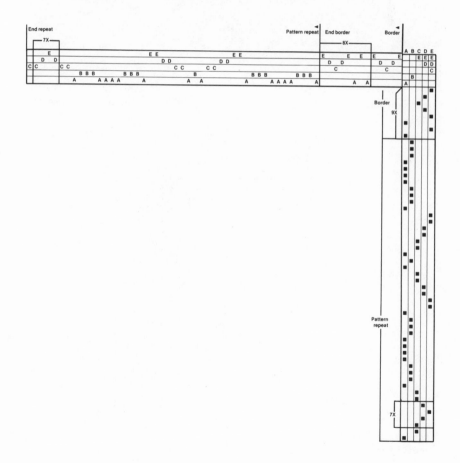

179

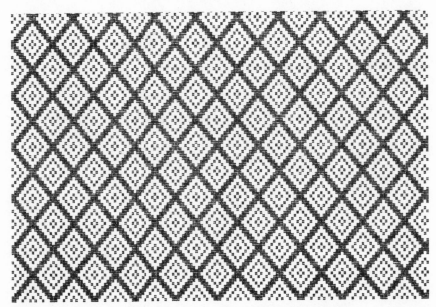

This is the small, multicolored fragment on the top of the blue-and-white coverlet on page 40.

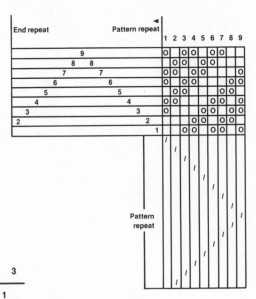

End repeat   Pattern repeat

Pattern repeat

TIE-UP: Nearly $\dfrac{2\quad3}{3\quad1}$

TREADLING: As drawn in
16 ends in pattern repeat.

180

Diamonds or Goose Eye plaid. Goose Eye is fine diamonds within heavier diamonds.

WARP COUNT: 25 e.p.i.

WARP & WEFT: Single-ply (S-twist) wool, gray blue, coral red, and olive green in stripes and bands of 8, 32, and 48 ends.

SIZE: Fragment 10" wide by 10½" long (25.4 x 26.6 cm) plus fringes.

NOTES: The fragment has raveled ½" (1.2 cm) fringes on all four edges, whip-stitched with light blue sewing thread. It is in excellent condition.

COLOR ORDER (partial, as this is only a fragment):

WARP

gray blue		48			8	8
coral red				32		8
olive green	32		32	8		

WEFT

gray blue	48		
coral red		64	
olive green	32		32

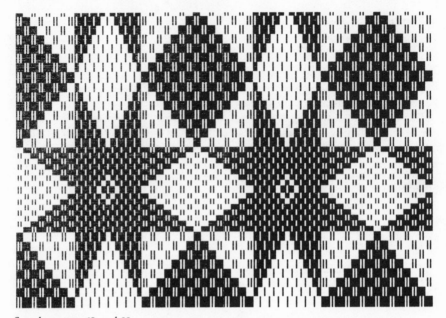

See also pages 62 and 83.

TIE-UP: For star and diamond, with ties used alternately
TREADLING: Nearly as drawn in
120 ends in pattern repeat

Star & Diamond. Eight-pointed stars point-to-point with solid diamonds.

WARP COUNT: 27 e.p.i.

WARP: Two-ply (Z-twist S-ply) cotton, natural.

WEFTS: *Tabby:* Fine single-ply (Z-twist) cotton, natural. *Pattern:* Two-ply (Z-twist S-ply) wool, dark blue and uneven light yellowish brown.

SIZE: Irregular fragment 14" wide by 10½" long (36 x 27 cm); 2 by 1½ repeats.

NOTES: This weave structure is similar to summer & winter, because there are two tie-down shafts. Some of the units are three ends wide and some are five. The pattern skips are woven in blocks, rather than in singles or pairs as they would be in summer & winter. The fragment has the remains of a narrow hem at the top, a selvedge on one side, a cut bottom, and an irregularly torn edge on the other side. It is very worn. It came from a Pennsylvania collector who had acquired it in Chambersburg, Pennsylvania.

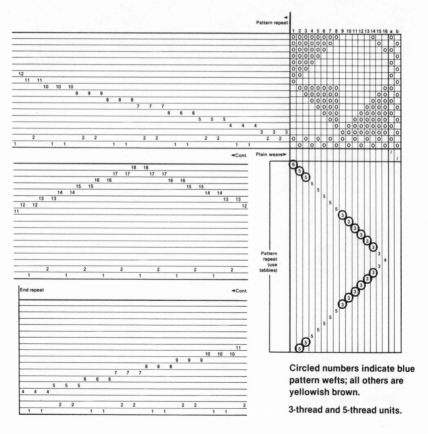

Circled numbers indicate blue pattern wefts; all others are yellowish brown.

3-thread and 5-thread units.

183

See also pages 40 and 53 (on page 40, this is the blue and red coverlet at left center).

TIE-UP: Irregular, with two of the four ties used at a time
TREADLING: Nearly as drawn in
196 ends in pattern repeat; border not given in threading or treadling.

Tulips, Roses, and Snowball, with Tree border. A double tulip motif, surrounded by a rectangular frame, alternated with a solid snowball (which forms a semi-ringed rose between the rectangles).

WARP COUNT: 36 e.p.i.

WARP: Fine single-ply (Z-twist) cotton, natural.

WEFTS: *Tabby:* Same as warp. *Pattern:* Two-ply (Z-twist S-ply) wool, coral red and dark blue.

SIZE: 66″ (168 cm) and two fringes wide by 78″ (198 cm) and one fringe long; 10½ repeats and two borders by 13 repeats and one border.

NOTES: This unusual threading is like a tied unit weave, but the four tie-downs are not used in a regular formula order. The effect is like a combination of repeat twill or overshot and tied weaves.

The coverlet is two panels (one seam, well matched). The top is a narrow hem; the sides (selvedges) and bottom (narrow hem) have added tape-woven fringe with three-ply (Z-twist S-ply) white cotton warp, and wefts of white three-ply (Z-twist S-ply) cotton and the same red and blue wools as the coverlet. The coverlet is in poor condition; it is very worn, torn, and mended.

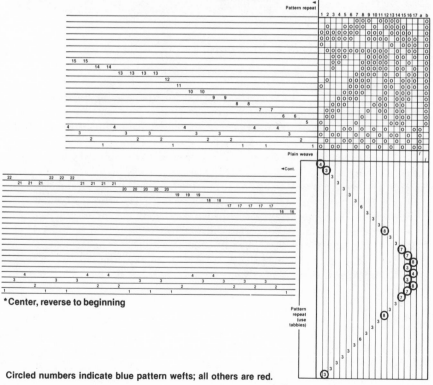

*Center, reverse to beginning

Circled numbers indicate blue pattern wefts; all others are red.

185

Double Rose, with Leaf & Vine border.

WARP COUNT: 32 e.p.i.

WARPS: *Ground:* Two-ply (Z-twist S-ply) cotton, yellowed natural. *Tie-downs:* Fine single-ply (Z-twist) cotton, pale blue.

WEFTS: *Tabby:* Single-ply (Z-twist) cotton, yellowed natural. *Pattern:* Two-ply (Z-twist S-ply) wool, dark blue, dusky yellow-green, dark bright red, and rose-pink.

SIZE: 75" wide by 86" long (190 x 218 cm); 4 repeats and two borders by 5½ repeats and one border.

NOTES: This pattern is very similar or identical to Swygert pp. 322-27 and 386. The coverlet is in two panels (one seam). The top is a narrow hem; the bottom is a slightly wider flat hem with a raw upper edge. The bands of color are well matched to the pattern motifs. The corner inscription reads *MADE BY SAMUEL MELLINGER 1839. Checklist* . . . identifies Samuel Mellinger as having woven with Emanuel Meily, Jr., and John Mellinger in Lebanon County, Pennsylvania, in 1834, and in Lancaster County, Pennsylvania, in 1850. *See also page 66.*

186

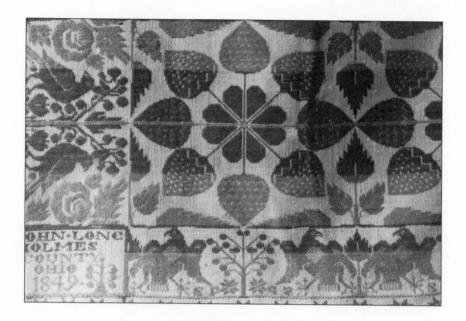

Strawberries, with Bird & Rose and Eagle borders.

WARP COUNT: 33 e.p.i. (22 ground, 11 tie-down).
WARPS: *Ground and tie-down:* Uneven single-ply (Z-twist) cotton, yellowed natural.
WEFTS: *Tabby:* Same as warps. *Pattern:* Two-ply (Z-twist S-ply) wool, unevenly faded coral red and avocado green.
SIZE: 78″ (198 cm) and two fringes wide by 81″ (206 cm) long; 4 repeats and two borders by 5¾ repeats and one border.
NOTES: This coverlet is in two panels (one seam, well matched). The top and bottom edges have been torn off. The top edge probably had a narrow hem and the bottom edge was likely a warp fringe, made with both warps. The sides are the remains of a 2½″ (6 cm) loop fringe of pattern wefts. The coverlet is in fair condition, whole but worn and very dry.

The corner signature panel reads *JOHN LONG / HOLMES COUNTY / OHIO / 1849.* The eagle border contains the initials *SP. Checklist . . .* (p. 82) lists John Long as weaving in Holmes County, Ohio, from 1840 to 1855. The central pattern of this coverlet is very unusual, although it has a leaf element that is common in some Bird or Eagle borders. Shortly before this coverlet was purchased, another one by the same weaver was documented in the stock of an Indiana dealer. It was identical to this one, except for color (dark blue and white), condition (excellent), and date (1854).

See also pages 40, 86, and 90 (on page 40 this is the beige, red, and green coverlet in the center).

Unnamed "carnation & tulip" medallion, with Rose border.

WARP COUNT: 33 e.p.i. (22 ground/light layer and 11 tie-down/dark layer).

WARPS: *Ground:* Heavy three-ply (Z-twist S-ply) cotton, natural. *Tie-down:* Single-ply (Z-twist) cotton, light blue.

WEFTS: *Ground:* Fine single-ply (Z-twist) cotton, natural. *Pattern:* Two-ply (Z-twist S-ply) wool, dark blue, dusky rose, and mustard.

SIZE: 80" wide by 82" long (203 x 208 cm); 4 repeats and two borders by 4 repeats and one border.

NOTES: This coverlet is seamless. The top and bottom are torn; the sides are selvedges. The tied doublecloth is partly double weave (two threads in the light layer for every one in the dark) and partly Jacquard single (two ground threads and one tie-down thread in a unit). The corner reads *MADE BY G. NICKLAS / CHAMBERSBURGH* [sic] / *FRANKLIN COUNTY 18[?]0* (probably 1860). The Gs look like Cs, and the 6 is incomplete in the date. *Checklist . . .* says George Nicklas, a German immigrant, was listed in the census as a carpet weaver in Chambersburg, Franklin County, Pennsylvania. The authors recorded fourteen of his coverlets, dated 1840 to 1860.

Except for color and date, this coverlet is identical to Swygert p. 348 and almost identical to Davison & Mayer-Thurman #126, which was woven by an Ohio weaver who learned in Franklin County, Pennsylvania. The weaver is listed in *Checklist . . .* (p. 93) and is also found in Swygert (pp. 327, 348). The central design (of what I call the carnation & tulip medallion) is similar to the designs in many coverlets shown in Swygert, and the border (which is the very common Bird & Rose border, without the birds) is also widely found. *See also pages 39, 49, 52, and 86.*

Center medallion with Capitol, deer, and wild turkey border.

WARP COUNT: 27 e.p.i. (18 natural & 9 blue).

WARPS: *Background layer:* Three-ply (Z-twist S-ply) cotton, natural. *Pattern layer:* Single-ply (Z-twist) cotton, light blue.

WEFTS: *Background layer:* Heavy single-ply (Z-twist) cotton. *Pattern layer:* Three-ply (Z-twist S-ply) wool, dark blue and rose and dark mustard and pale green (all faded).

SIZE: 79" wide by 76" long (200 x 193 cm) (1 repeat & 2 borders by 1 repeat & 2 borders).

NOTES: The coverlet is almost identical to Burnham #473 and Swygert p. 370. It is seamless. Top is a narrow hem; sides have remnants of approximately 2" (5 cm) pattern-weft fringe; bottom is remnants of tape-woven fringe to match (natural cotton warp, colored wool fringe). Condition is fairly good; coverlet is worn but whole. Coverlet is a family heirloom. Owner's mother-in-law said it had belonged to her grandmother, and she remembered seeing it on her grandmother's bed when she was a child. She therefore thought it dated to the 1840s. She was born in the late 1870s; the coverlet may have been new when she was a child. Several features of the coverlet (the single center motif, the "Victorian" representations of animals and buildings, the seamlessness, the "sleazy" unbalanced weave and imbalance in thread sizes, and the combination of natural and synthetic colors) indicate that this is probably a late 19th-century coverlet, from the Centennial-inspired revival or later (1875-1900). *See also page 15.*

Peacocks Feeding Young, with Old Boston Town double border.

WARP COUNT: 38 e.p.i. (19 in each surface).
WARPS & WEFTS: *Light layer:* Two-ply (Z-twist S-ply) cotton, natural. *Dark layer:* Two-ply (Z-twist S-ply) wool, dark blue.
SIZE: 74" (188 cm) and two fringes wide by 95" (241 cm) and one fringe long; 3 repeats and two double borders by 4 repeats and two borders, one double and one single.
NOTES: This pattern and its border are common, almost identical to Swygert p. 238, DeGraw #127-28, and Davison & Mayer-Thurman #115. The coverlet is in two panels (one seam). The bottom has warp fringe (both warps); the sides have weft fringe (cotton layer only); the top has cut edges overcast in cross-stitch using the dark blue wool thread. A few "specks" indicate the weaver was using worn cards. There is no signature block. The coverlet is in excellent condition.
See also page 66.

Frenchman's Fancy, with Peacocks and Floral borders.

WARP COUNT: 36 e.p.i. (18 in each layer).

WARPS & WEFTS: *Light layer:* Three-ply (Z-twist S-ply) cotton, yellowed natural. *Dark layer:* Two-ply (Z-twist S-ply) wool, dark blue and brick red.

SIZE: 76" (193 cm) wide by 90" (229 cm) and fringe long; 3 repeats and two borders by 3½ repeats and one border.

NOTES: This pattern is one of two different designs called Frenchman's Fancy by different authors. The peacocks in the side border are the same birds that appear in the central design of the common Peacocks Feeding Young pattern. The entire coverlet is identical, except for color, date, and weaver, to Swygert p. 284. The central design, of six roses and a plumed medallion, is also similar to Montgomery pp. 62 and 110 (also on the paper jacket). The bottom floral border is the same as in Montgomery plates IX and XI, and similar to plate X and to Hall p. 309 (these are all coverlets by the LaTourette family). The side border is also similar to borders on coverlets in Montgomery. The corner of this piece reads *YEAR 1852*, the trademark of Sarah and Henry LaTourette, who assumed the Fountain County, Indiana, weaving business of their father, John, when he died in 1849. (See *Checklist . . .* p. 78 and Montgomery pp. 67-69 for details about this weaving family.)

This coverlet is in two panels (one seam, well matched). The top is torn off; the bottom is the remains of warp fringe, originally 4" (10 cm) long; the sides are selvedges (interlocked wefts). The stripes and bands of red and blue are very well fitted to the design. An occasional flaw indicates worn punch-cards, which is quite possible, since the pattern is identical to a coverlet John LaTourette wove several years earlier. *See also pages 21, 38, and 54.*

Unnamed floral medallion.

WARP COUNT: 38 e.p.i. (19 in each layer).

WARPS & WEFTS: *Light layer:* Four-ply (Z-twist S-ply) cotton, natural. *Dark layer:* Two-ply (Z-twist S-ply) wool, dark blue and pinkish rose.

SIZE: 70" wide by 58½" long (178 x 149 cm); 3 by 2 repeats.

NOTES: This coverlet is in two panels (one seam, well matched). The pattern is almost identical to Swygert p. 311 and to Davison & Mayer-Thurman #101. The design has no borders (both illustrations listed have only a narrow line frame). Both ends are cut off, machine-stitched, and hemmed; the sides appear to have been cut off and hand overcast-stitched with a Z-ply thread, and machine stay-stitched. The Davison & Mayer-Thurman reference attributes its coverlet #101 to Waynesburg, Greene County, Pennsylvania, in 1849.

    The coverlet is fairly whole; the cotton layer is worn, and holes have been patched and mended. The piece is a family heirloom. The family says it was woven by George Lehr (1795-1871), of whom they have a portrait. According to family histories, George Lehr was born July 2, 1795, in Mountainville, Lehigh County, Pennsylvania. He and his wife, Salome Lessig Lehr, moved to an area which is now Mahoning County, where his eleventh child (Henry) was born in 1838. The family moved to New Baltimore, Stark County, Ohio, in 1840, and three years later to an area near Overton, in Wayne County, Ohio. It is known that George wove "carpets, flannels, coverlets, satinelles, etc." there. He is said to be buried "on the north side of Lehman Cemetery." At least one of his sons, Daniel, is thought to have been a weaver, too; newspaper clippings in the family possession show an 1848 piece signed by Daniel, of Dalton, Wayne County, and several other pieces attributed to him. *See also page 65.*

Unnamed, with Train border.

WARP COUNT: 36 e.p.i. (18 in each layer).

WARPS & WEFTS: *Light layer:* Two-ply (Z-twist S-ply) cotton, natural. *Dark layer:* Two-ply (Z-twist S-ply) wool, dark blue.

SIZE: 79" (201 cm) plus fringes wide by 87" (221 cm) plus fringe long.

NOTES: The coverlet is in two panels (one seam). It has warp fringe (made with both warps) on the bottom, weft fringe (including both wefts) on the sides. The top was originally finished by turning both layers to the inside and overcasting the two folds together; it was later covered with a brown and red printed cotton bias binding, which has faded and deteriorated.

The pattern of the coverlet center is a conglomeration of seven different motifs, three of which also appear in a Michigan-owned coverlet with a similar border. The four-petaled corner motif and the small scroll frame are different from any seen in print so far, although the corner is almost identical to that on the Michigan-owned coverlet.

The Train border on both of these coverlets is similar to, yet different from, that on the "Hemfield Railroad commemorative" coverlets shown in Swygert p. 229 and Safford & Bishop pp. 264-65. The commemorative coverlets (which feature the words *HEMFIELD RAILROAD* framing a portrait in the corners) are thought to refer to a small, partially completed line in southwestern Pennsylvania, and are apparently not as rare as was once thought. It seems that their only relationship to this coverlet is in the similarity of the borders.

There are many differences in small details, such as the engine and tender wheels, the lumps of coal in the tender, and the tracks and ties. There are two major

193

differences between this coverlet and the others. This one has an additional car labeled *PIQUA No. 241* in the side borders only, and the trains in the side borders all point in the same direction (from the top toward the foot). In all of the others, including the bottom border of this piece, the trains are only engine and tender (labeled *No. 240*) and are nose-to-nose.

This piece has no indication of weaver or date, but the style indicates western Ohio about 1850. The flower, leaf, and grapevine border at the top (badly tattered) reads *PIQUA O.* in the frame. It is assumed that this refers to Piqua, Miami County, Ohio. An Ohio railroad historian points out that there was a locomotive named PIQUA which was used on the Columbus, Piqua and Indiana Railroad from about 1852 to 1870, but that the engine was of a different type. He suggests that the engine on this coverlet is similar to the JOHN BULL (which is now in the Smithsonian), and speculates that the weaver took his design from a standard printers' die which newspapers used in the 1850s. He finds no local Piqua correlation for the numbers 240 and 241.

From all of this, it is fair to assume that the unknown weaver of this coverlet either bought prepunched cards or copied a design for the lower border and then punched his own cards for the side borders and central design (which is asymmetrical to coincide with the one-directional trains). *See also page 67.*

Bibliography

Primary books for further reading

Burnham, Harold B. and Dorothy K. 'Keep Me Warm One Night': Early Handweaving in Eastern Canada. Toronto: University of Toronto Press, 1972. Well-written book, with clear diagrams of weave structures, drafts for every fabric (mostly coverlets), detailed fabric analyses, and historical information. Although entirely Canadian, closely related to a large portion of eastern American weaving.

Heisey, John W., compiler. A Checklist of American Coverlet Weavers. Williamsburg, Virginia: Colonial Williamsburg Foundation, 1978. Excellent compilation of known information about 19th-century professional weavers and their coverlets. Includes geographical information, brief biographies, and pictures of known "trademark" signature blocks.

Montgomery, Pauline. Indiana Coverlet Weavers and Their Coverlets. Indianapolis, Indiana: Hoosier Heritage Press, 1974. Biographies of Indiana professional (Jacquard) weavers. Limited in scope but with deep coverage of its subject. Concentrates on the weavers, not the weavings.

Swygert, Mrs. Luther M. Heirlooms from Old Looms: A Catalogue of Coverlets Owned by The Colonial Coverlet Guild of America and its Members. Chicago: CCGA, 1955. Entirely black-and-white photos, with some pattern names (and a very little mis-classification); no technical details on any coverlets. Useful primarily for the variety of coverlets pictured.

Wilson, Sadye Tune, and Kennedy, Doris Finch. Of Coverlets; the Legacies, the Weavers. Nashville, Tennessee: Tunstede, 1983. A monumental study of coverlets (mostly overshot) documented in the Tennessee Textile History Project 1978-83. Liberally illustrated with color and black-and-white photos of coverlets and their weavers. Includes complete technical information.

Additional relevant volumes

Note: Some of these are exhibition catalogs, some are monographs or books on aspects of early American textiles, and some are books written primarily for weavers. Many of them are long out-of-print.

Adrosko, Rita J. Natural Dyes and Home Dyeing. New York: Dover, 1971.

Atwater, Mary Meigs. The Shuttle-craft Book of American Hand-weaving. Coupeville, Washington: Shuttle-craft Books, 1986 (originally 1951).

Channing, Marion L. The Textile Tools of Colonial Homes. Marion, Massachusetts: Marion L. Channing, 1971.

Conley, Emma, Vegetable Dying [sic]. Penland, North Carolina: Penland School of Handicrafts, 1959?

Cooper, Grace Rogers. The Copp Family Textiles. Washington, D.C.: Smithsonian Institution Press, 1971.

Coverlets in the Collection of the Chester County Historical Society. West Chester, Pennsylvania: Chester County Historical Society, 1976.

Davison, Marguerite Porter. Pennsylvania German Home Weaving (Home Craft Course v. 4). Plymouth Meeting, Pennsylvania: Mrs. C. Naaman Keyser, 1947.

Davison, Mildred, and Mayer-Thurman, Christa C. *Coverlets: A Handbook on the Collection.* . . . Chicago: Art Institute of Chicago, 1973.

DeGraw, Imelda G. *Quilts and Coverlets.* Denver: The Denver Art Museum, 1974.

Dolan, J.R. *The Yankee Peddlers of Early America.* New York: Bramhall House, 1964.

Earle, Alice Morse. *Home Life in Colonial Days.* Middle Village, New York: Jonathan David Publishers, 1975 (originally 1898).

The Eckert Collection of American Coverlets: An Exhibition. . . . Anderson, Indiana: Fine Arts Center, 1978.

Fennelly, Catherine. *Textiles in New England, 1790-1840.* Sturbridge, Massachusetts: Old Sturbridge Village, 1961.

Finch, Karen, and Putnam, Greta. *Caring for Textiles.* New York: Watson-Guptill, 1977.

Fiske, Patricia L., ed. *Imported and Domestic Textiles in 18th-century America* (Proceedings of 1975 Irene Emery Roundtable on Museum Textiles). Washington, D.C.: The Textile Museum, 1975.

Gehret, Ellen J., and Keyser, Alan G. *The Homespun Textile Tradition of the Pennsylvania Germans.* N.p.: Pennsylvania Farm Museum of Landis Valley, 1976.

Hall, Eliza Calvert. *A Book of Hand-woven Coverlets.* Rutland, Vermont: Tuttle, 1966 (originally 1912).

Homespun to Factory Made: Woolen Textiles in America, 1776-1876. North Andover, Massachusetts: Merrimack Valley Textile Museum, 1977.

Linen-Making in New England, 1640-1860. North Andover, Massachusetts: Merrimack Valley Textile Museum, 1980.

Mailand, Harold F. *Considerations for the Care of Textiles and Costumes: A Handbook for the Non-specialist.* Indianapolis, Indiana: Indianapolis Museum of Art, 1980.

Montgomery, Florence M. *Textiles in America 1650-1870: A Dictionary.* . . . New York: Norton, 1983.

Pennington, David A., and Taylor, Michael B. *A Pictorial Guide to American Spinning Wheels.* Sabbathday Lake, Maine: Shaker Press, 1975.

Prized Possessions: 19th-century Woven Coverlets from the Collection of Ken Colwell. Rockford, Illinois: Rockford Art Association, 1978.

Reinert, Guy F. *Pennsylvania German Coverlets* (Home Craft Course v. 9). Plymouth Meeting, Pennsylvania: Mrs. C. Naaman Keyser, 1947.

Safford, Carleton L., and Bishop, Robert. *America's Quilts and Coverlets.* New York: Dutton, 1972.

Safner, Isadora, and Piette, Diane. *The Weaving Book of Peace and Patience.* Brewster, Massachusetts: Two Cape Cod Weavers, 1980.

Safner, Isadora. *The Weaving Roses of Rhode Island.* Loveland, Colorado: Interweave Press, 1985.

Schorsch, Anita, ed. *The Art of the Weaver.* New York: Universe Books, 1977.

Strickler, Carol. *A Portfolio of American Coverlets.* 5 vol. Boulder, Colorado: Carol Strickler, 1978-83.

Tate, Lou. *Kentucky Coverlets.* Louisville, Kentucky: Lou Tate, 1938.

Walker, Sandra Rambo. *Country Cloth to Coverlets: Textile Traditions in 19th-century Central Pennsylvania.* Lewisburg, Pennsylvania: Oral Traditions Project of Union County (PA) Historical Society, 1981.

Wilson, Kax. *A History of Textiles.* Boulder, Colorado: Westview Press, 1979.

Worst, Edward F. *Weaving with Foot-power Looms.* New York: Dover, 1974 (originally 1918).

Index